i

TABLE OF CONTENTS

LIST OF FIGURES

ABSTRACT

The main objective of the dissertation is to present work describing theoretical studies of planar structures with erbium doped regions and characterization of erbium doped particles. Numerical models of erbium doped Al_2O_3 were formulated, taking into account the up-conversion from the metastable Er^{3+} levels and the cross-relaxation process as a mechanism of energy transfer between Er^{3+} ions. The influence of amplified spontaneous emission (ASE) is also fully considered in the numerical model.

The first part of this research investigates the effects of design geometries and nonlinear losses on gain in silicon waveguides with multiple trenched erbium-doped Al_2O_3 regions. Distributing erbium ions over multi-trench areas improves the gain to nonlinear loss ratio. 0.38 dB/cm higher signal amplification was generated when comparing the multiple and single-trench configurations.

In the second part of this work, a dielectric vertical emitter structure consisting of an erbium doped active material layer sandwiched between two metallic layers is studied. In this structure, metal layers are used to guide the plasmonic pump mode that has the role of exciting the active material and act as mirrors in the vertical direction to form a cavity resonating at 1532 nm. We employ the transverse resonance method to compute the modes in the structure, and we focus on even (with respect to the x polarized electric field) TM modes. We show that such structures can be promising candidates for dielectric based vertical emitters.

In the last part of this dissertation, characterization of micron sized erbium doped particles is discussed. We demonstrate the feasibility of single-shot, single-detector high-resolution imaging and tracking by a time–space-wavelength mapping technique. We experimentally demonstrate single-shot imaging at 1 line/50 ns capture rate. A correlation method is implemented to obtain the transient movement of an individual particle. This system can be further optimized for real-time imaging, tracking of multiple micro-particles or arbitrary objects.

Chapter 1

Introduction

1.1. Introduction

During the past few decades, fiber optical communication systems have demonstrated an unprecedented potential for high-capacity and high-speed data transmission. Fiber optic communication systems contain several optical components, such as amplifiers, lasers, modulators, multiplexers, splitters, and detectors, connected by optical fibers. Modern commercial optical silica fibers are capable of transmitting 10 to 40 GB/s at one signal wavelength, while up to 80 signal channels can be embedded in a single fiber link. In the wavelength region of 1.5 μm, one of the standard wavelengths used in optical telecommunication, modern fibers exhibit losses as low as 0.3 dB/km [1].

A significant reduction in system size and cost can be achieved by the development of integrated optics to replace some of the discrete components used in fiber optical communication systems. Recently, developments of integrated optics are being intensively investigated, in which several optical functions are performed on a single substrate. An extremely large amount of data can travel at the telecommunication wavelength 1.5μm in a very small space, making integrated optics very attractive. In circuits with integrated optics, light is directed to different optical components through planar optical waveguides. One of the ideal candidates for integrated optical circuits is silicon, due to the low cost silicon wafers and the capability of monolithic integration of optical and electronic circuits. In the last few years, efforts have been directed more towards silicon based active photonic devices such as amplifiers, and light emitters [2]. Achieving gain in silicon has been one of the most challenging goals due to the nature of the indirect bandgap of silicon. Recently, several attempts have been made to incorporate gain materials such as erbium into silicon to achieve optical gain at telecommunication wavelengths [3].

The internal atomic transitions at 1.54 μm of erbium ions are exploited to achieve light amplification at telecommunication wavelengths. Using an external laser source, optical pumping is introduced to excite the Er^{3+} ions and ensure the population inversion needed to achieve optical amplification. Erbium doped fiber amplifiers (EDFAs) which were first presented in 1987 represent one successful solution for all-optical signal amplification. The planar analogy of EDFAs, erbium doped waveguide amplifiers (EDWA) has also been investigated intensively in the past few years [4]. In EDWAs the signal enhancement is achieved in a few cm long, highly doped waveguide, which can be integrated with other functions to produce lossless and small-sized network components. One of the most remarkable erbium doped waveguide amplifiers developed was based on an Al$_2$O$_3$ substrate [5]. It provided a net gain of 2.3 dB when pumped with a 9-mW pump laser at 1480 nm. In addition, efficient waveguide amplifiers with high gain per unit length have been demonstrated based on silicate and phosphate glass substrates [6] .

Despite the successes of using different host materials such as silica, glass and Al$_2$O$_3$ etc., the use of silicon as a host material for erbium to achieve optical gain at 1.54μm has been challenging. Erbium luminescence in crystalline silicon has only been observed at low temperatures. Because of the scattering losses and fabrication complexities of the nanoparticles, erbium doped crystalline silicon is not considered a promising candidate to achieve optical gain [3]. Thus the still-open question is how to achieve optical gain by incorporating erbium into the silicon based structures more efficiently.

Recently, erbium doped gain mediums have also attracted research interest in the field of plasmonics. The use of plasmonics mixed with active photonic materials has been found to be promising since the gain experienced through the emission of a gain medium is capable of counteracting the high attenuation of the electromagnetic wave. Loss compensation of surface plasmon-polaritons (SPPs) is important for integrated devices coupling both electronic and photonic data transmissions as well as SPP amplifiers and SPP lasers [7]. Direct experimental evidence of stimulated emission of surface plasmon-polaritons (SPPs) at telecom wavelengths (1532 nm) with erbium doped glass as a gain medium has been presented [8]. Yet signal enhancement and loss compensation of signal surface plasmons is still difficult to be achieved due to the limited signal enhancement due to metal losses, and to thermal effects. However, the unique features of surface plasmons, such as enhanced and spatially confined electromagnetic fields at metal dielectric interfaces, can been exploited for exciting erbium doped gain mediums. In addition, the unique features of metal layers in the plasmonic structures can act as mirrors which can form a resonating cavity. Thus, there is an interest in investigating plasmonic structures with metal and erbium doped gain materials for dielectric based vertical emitters and resonant cavities.

In another field of interest, characterization of submicron particles such as Er^{3+} doped silica particles has been extensively investigated. Different laser scanning microscopes including fluorescence or scattering based mechanisms have been proposed and illustrated for obtaining high-resolution optical images for submicron sized particles [9]. Unfortunately, it is difficult to improve temporal resolutions to less than a few

3

microseconds due the limitation of data acquisition speeds of detector arrays. In recent years, a unique solution called time-wavelength mapping has been proposed to improve temporal resolution and to realize real-time optical measurements using a single-detector and single-shot measurement [10]. This technique has recently been implemented to detect highly reflective objects with sub-gigahertz resolution. The time-wavelength mapping technique also prevails over the slow-speed conventional spectrometers and allows real-time single-shot measurements of dynamic processes. Thus, there is a need to integrate the time-wavelength mapping technique with a suitable image technique to provide real-time optical imaging and tracking of submicron sized particles. This technique can be potentially applied to vitro biological samples, and to capture transient properties of target objects in electro-mechanics.

1.2. Scope of this dissertation

The work presented in this dissertation has been divided into five chapters:

Chapter 1 contains a brief introduction and describes the aims and motivations of this research.

Chapter 2 presents an overview of spectroscopic properties of Er^{3+}. Energy levels and fundamental properties of Er^{3+} including energy transfer processes have been discussed in details. Also, different host materials for Er^{3+} are introduced. This chapter provides a background for the subsequent chapters.

Chapter 3 provides a theoretical study of silicon waveguides with multiple Er^{3+} doped regions. We discuss the physics models for Er^{3+} and silicon as well as the amplification process of Er^{3+} and the signal evolving process in the structure. We also discuss the effects of structure designs, nonlinear and linear loss mechanisms in both Er^{3+} doped Al_2O_3 and silicon on the optical gain.

Chapter 4 introduces a design of an erbium-based plasmonic-assisted vertical emitter. Models of Er^{3+} and metal used in the structure are discussed. Subsequently, we optimize the proposed structures based on the effects of the physical parameters for Er^{3+} and metal to achieve a net gain.

Chapter 5 demonstrates a system to characterize micron sized Er^{3+} doped particles. Techniques including space-wavelength mapping and time-wavelength mapping have been introduced to achieve space-time-wavelength mapping used in this system. Image correlation spectroscopy has also been introduced for image post-processing. We experientially demonstrate a single-shot, single-detector, high-resolution, imaging and tracking by time–space-wavelength mapping technique. We show that 1 line/50 ns capture rate can be achieved.

Chapter 2

Spectroscopic properties of Er³⁺

The specific spectroscopic feature of Er³⁺ ions is that they facilitate a strong radiative transition in the 1.54 µm wavelength region, which matches the operation bandwidth of the contemporary transmission systems. This chapter is a detailed discussion of the atomic physics of Er³⁺ and is provided as a background for following chapters. In this chapter, fundamental atomic properties of erbium ions and the optical properties that result from a variety of host materials are discussed.

In section 2.1 we will examine the associated energy levels and optical spectra of Er³⁺. Then, in section 2.2 we will discuss different host materials for Er³⁺ and their impact on the optical properties. In section 2.3, we will discuss the spectroscopic fundamentals including the transition cross sections and the transition rates, which will be used in subsequent chapters. Finally, in section 2.4, we will discuss the energy transfer processes including ion-ion interaction effects which play importance roles in optical amplification.

2.1. Energy levels of Er³⁺

Erbium is a rare earth element belonging to the group of the Lanthanides. When embedded in a solid, erbium generally assumes the trivalent Er³⁺ state, which has an electronic configuration [Xe]-4f¹¹. The Er³⁺ ion has an incompletely filled 4f-shell, allowing for different electronic configurations with different energies due to spin-spin and spin-orbit interactions [11]. Radiative transitions between most of these energy levels are parity forbidden for free Er³⁺ ions. When Er³⁺ ions are incorporated in a solid however, the surrounding material perturbs the 4f wave functions. This has two important consequences. Firstly, the host material can introduce odd-parity character in the Er 4f wave functions, making radiative transitions weakly allowed. Secondly, the host material causes Stark-splitting of the different energy levels, which results in a broadening of the optical transitions. Figure 1 shows a schematic level diagram of the Stark-split Er^{3+} energy levels, labeled using Russell-Saunders notation.

The first excited state denoted as $^4I_{13/2}$ is metastable and enables a laser transition to the ground state peaking at the wavelength of 1.54 µm. In the thermodynamic equilibrium the majority of erbium ions are found in the ground state. However, to achieve optical gain, the condition of population inversion must be fulfilled, which assumes that more than a half of the Er^{3+} ions sit in higher energy levels. Using an external laser source, optical pumping is introduced to excite the Er^{3+} ions and ensure the population inversion. Deexcitation of the erbium ions can occur either spontaneously or by stimulated emission. In the ideal case, a signal photon of 1.54 µm traveling through the active medium stimulates the emission of a second photon, having the same frequency, phase, polarization and direction of propagation as the original one. This process results in the signal amplification. Spontaneous deexcitation can proceed either radiatively or nonradiatively. The radiative spontaneous emission produces photons with random phase, polarization and propagation direction which, especially when further amplified, are the source of amplifier noise. Furthermore, the spontaneous emission decreases the population inversion and in general limits the amplifier gain.

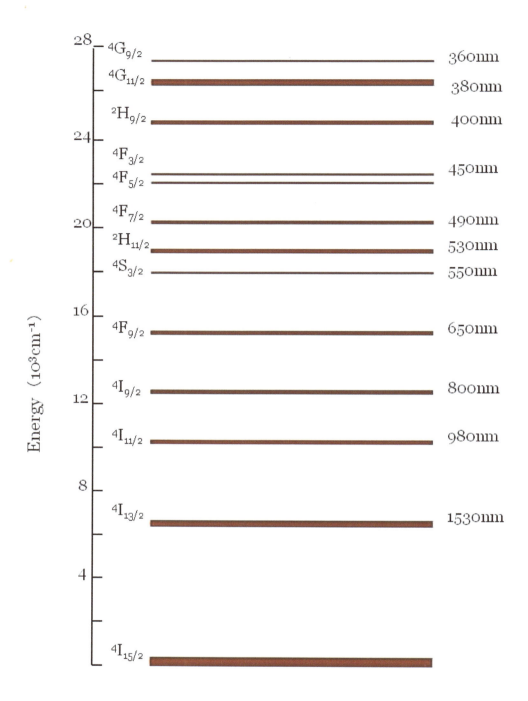

Figure 1. Schematic representation of the Stark-split Er³⁺ energy levels [11].

In accordance with the Judd-Ofelt theory [12, 13], optical spectrum of Er^{3+} is mainly caused by the 4f inner-shell electronic transitions, therefore radiative 4f transitions between the states can be produced. Figure 2 shows the absorption spectra of Er^{3+} in the Er-doped Al_2O_3 thin film (prepared by sputtering deposition and ion implantation) [14]. From the energy level structure of Er^{3+} and the absorption spectrum analysis, several wavelengths can be used as pump sources including 0.514 μm (argon ion laser), 0.532 μm (SHG YAG laser), 0.665 μm (dye laser), 0.82 μm (semiconductor laser), 0.98 μm (semiconductor laser), and 1.48μm (semiconductor laser).

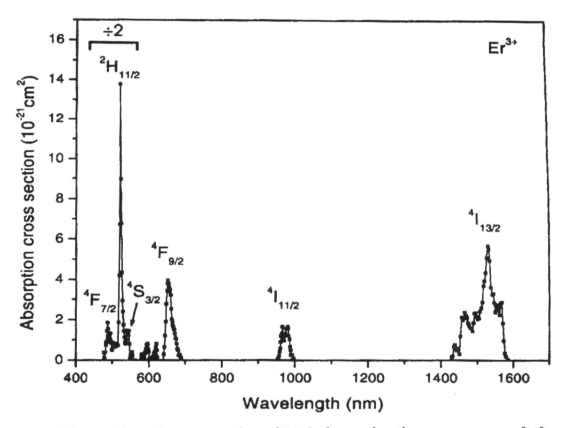

Figure 2 Absorption cross-sections of Er^{3+} in the wavelength range 0.4-1.70 μm [14].

2.2 Host materials

9

A variety of different host materials are used for Er-doped fiber amplifiers and planar waveguide devices. Er-doped optical fiber amplifiers are predominately made of silica-based glasses. Al is co-doped in the fiber to increase the solubility of Er^{3+} ions. Furthermore, a wide choice can be made, in the balance between Er^{3+} concentration in the fiber and the fiber length. It has been shown that an efficient Er-doped fiber amplifier can be achieved with an Er concentration of $\sim10^{18}$ ions/cm^3 and a fiber length of a few tens of meters.

The main advantage of erbium doped waveguide amplifiers over their fiber counterpart is that they provide high gain in short optical paths. For comparison, while the length of a typical Erbium doped Fiber Amplifier (EDFA) is 10 to 50 meters, a waveguide amplifier needs to be only a few cm long to reach the same net gain. Such a high gain factor can be only achieved if the concentration of Er dopants is extremely high; more than of two orders higher than in fiber amplifiers. The materials used as substrates for waveguide amplifiers must fulfill three basic requirements:

(1) Be transparent at both signal and pump wavelengths

(2) Exhibit high solubility for Er^{3+} ions

(3) Allow for high quality waveguide fabrication

Until now, amorphous and crystalline materials have been explored for Er-doped planar waveguide amplifiers, including Al/P codoped silica [15], multi-component oxide glasses [16, 17], Al_2O_3 [18], $LiNbO_3$ [19] etc. Different materials are accompanied by different waveguide fabrication processes. Recently, other materials such as polymers, Si single-crystals and photonic crystals have been studied and tested as potential integrated laser or amplifier substrates.

The spectrum of Er^{3+} depends on the host materials [11]. The peaks and valleys in the spectra have different shapes based on the precise location of the Stark levels, the intensities of the transitions between the Stark levels, and on the amount of inhomogeneous and homogeneous broadening of these levels. Thus, absorption and emission spectra of Er^{3+} vary based on the different host materials. Therefore, the absorption and emission cross sections for the $^4I_{13/2}$ to $^4I_{15/2}$ transition also vary for different hosts. The host material composition also has a major effect on the lifetimes, radiative and nonradiative, of the excited states of Er^{3+} [11]. Nonradiative lifetimes depend largely on the nature of the glass or crystal host and the coupling between the vibrations of the lattice ions and the states of the rare earth ions. The lifetime of the Er^{3+} $^4I_{13/2}$ level, in various hosts can be found in [11].

2.3 Fundamental Properties of Er^{3+}

Quantitative analyses of optical amplifications of Er^{3+} in different host materials require parameters of fundamental properties of Er^{3+} to be known. Therefore, this section deals with the major fundamental properties of Er^{3+} that can be determined experimentally or theoretically.

2.3.1 Transition Cross Sections

The cross section of a transition between two states of an ion represents the probability for that transition to occur with emission or absorption of light. Absorption and emission cross-sections indicate the efficiency of optical pumping and signal amplification. The position of absorption peaks determine the most suitable wavelengths for optical pumping, while the emission peaks denote the possible signal bandwidths to be amplified. The absolute values of the cross-sections as well as the shape of their spectra strongly depend on the host matrix composition and hence the cross-sections have to be measured independently for each host material.

Absorption cross-section spectrum can be obtained from a direct transmission measurement. The measurement setup typically consists of a tunable monochromatic light source (e.g. a wolfram or Hg lamp with a monochromator) and a photodetector, which can cover both the visible and the infrared spectral range. When an Er^{3+} doped sample is illuminated with a beam of intensity $I_0(\lambda)$, the attenuation of the light intensity due to absorption can be expressed according to Lambert-Beer law:

$$I(L,\lambda) = I_0(\lambda)\exp(-\alpha(\lambda)L) \tag{1}$$

where $\alpha(\lambda)$ denotes the absorption coefficient and L is the thickness of the sample along the beam propagation direction. The absorption cross section $\sigma_a(\lambda)$ is then defined as the absorption coefficient $\alpha(\lambda)$ normalized to the Er^{3+} concentrations N and can be expressed as:

$$\sigma_a(\lambda) = \frac{\sigma(\lambda)}{N} = \frac{1}{NL}\ln\frac{I_o(\lambda)}{I(L,\lambda)}$$

(2)

Emission cross-section measurements are less straightforward and it is sufficient to give only relative results, contrary to the absorption measurement results. During the measurement, Er^{3+} ions are excited into higher energetic levels by optical pumping and at the same time the spontaneous emission in a desired wavelength range is detected. For Er^{3+} doped substrates the detection unit usually is comprised of a monochromator selecting the desired wavelength and a photodetector, which must be sensitive in the spectral interval of 1450 – 1650 nm.

In the next step, the measured relative emission spectrum must be properly scaled to yield the absolute emission cross-sections σ_e. If the metastable level lifetime is known, this could be done employing the relation [20]:

$$\frac{1}{\tau} = \frac{8\pi n^2}{c^2} \int_c v^2 \sigma_e(v)dv \tag{3}$$

where τ is the radiative lifetime, n the refractive index of the glass substrate c is the velocity of light and C denotes the spectral interval in which the Er^{3+} emission occurs.

However, absorption and emission cross section spectra are not independent of each other and it is often convenient to measure only one spectrum and calculate the other from the theory. One accepted procedure for relating the cross sections follows from the Einstein theory of spectral absorption and emission, generalized for a finite linewidth. The Einstein relationship is given by the expression:

$$g_1 \int v^2 \sigma_a^2(v)dv = g_2 \int v^2 \sigma_e^2(v)dv \tag{4}$$

Here g_1 and g_2 are the degeneracies of levels 1 and 2, v is the photon frequency and σ_a and σ_e are the frequency dependent absorption and emission cross sections. The generalized Einstein theory is valid, however, only if all components of the multiplets involved are equally populated, or all transitions have the same oscillator strengths. In most Er-doped host materials neither of the two conditions is fully satisfied, and therefore Einstein's approach does not necessarily provide accurate results.

An alternative technique relating σ_a and σ_e was presented by the McCumber theory [21]. The theory assumes that absorption and emission cross sections are connected by the detailed-balance relation:

$$\sigma_e(\nu) = \sigma_a(\nu) \exp(\frac{\varepsilon - h\nu}{KT}) \tag{5}$$

where ε is the excitation energy, i.e. the net free energy required to excite an erbium

ion from a lower to an upper energy level at a given temperature T. Note that even without

knowing the value of the excitation energy, by using equation (5) it is possible to calculate

the relative emission cross section spectra from $\sigma_a(\nu)$ and normalize them by means of Eq.

(3) and the measured lifetime.

To calculate the cross section spectra in absolute value, parameter ε has to be precisely

determined. Under the assumption of thermodynamic equilibrium the excitation energy

features in the following expression:

$$\frac{N_1}{N_2} = \exp(\frac{\varepsilon}{KT}) \tag{6}$$

which is the famous Boltzmann equation relating the rate of equilibrium occupancies N_1

and N_2 in a two level system at temperature T. In different erbium doped host materials,

however, the low symmetry crystal field lifts the degeneracy of the two energy levels and

to calculate the ratio N_1/N_2, one must know the positions of all the Stark level manifolds

containing multiple electronic sublevels with slightly different energies. Assuming g_1 is

the degeneracy of the ground state and g_2 the degeneracy of the excited state and N_1/N_2

can be expressed as [21]:

$$\frac{N_1}{N_2} = \frac{1 + \sum_{j=2}^{g_1/2} \exp(-\frac{E_{1j}}{KT})}{\exp(-\frac{E_0}{KT})[1 + \sum_{j=2}^{g_2/2} \exp(-\frac{E_{2j}}{KT})]} \tag{7}$$

where E_0 is the separation between the lowest components of each manifold and E_{ij} is the

difference in energy between the jth and the first component of level i. Although the fine electronic structure can be obtained from low temperature measurements of absorption and emission spectra, it is much more convenient and still accurate to consider a simplified electronic structure in which the Stark levels for a given manifold are equally spaced. This reduces the number of unknown parameters required in Eq. (7) from 14 to three: E_0 and the component spacing of each manifold ΔE_1, ΔE_2. Then the equation (7) simplifies to:

$$\frac{N_1}{N_2} = \exp(\frac{E_0}{KT}) \frac{1 - \exp(-\frac{\Delta E_2}{KT})}{1 - \exp(-\frac{\Delta E_1}{KT})} \frac{1 - \exp(-\frac{g_1 \Delta E_1}{2KT})}{1 - \exp(\frac{g_2 \Delta E_2}{2KT})} \tag{8}$$

A good estimate of unknown parameters E_0, ΔE_1 and ΔE_2 can be deduced from the shape of absorption and emission spectra. The highest absorption and emission peaks usually coincide and their position, as was confirmed by low-temperature spectroscopic measurements [22], corresponds to the energy separation E_0. Further, the bandwidth of the ground state, which equals $7 \cdot \Delta E_1$, is given by the energy difference of E_0 and the

lowest-energy component found in the emission spectrum. Similarly, $6 \cdot \Delta E_2$ can be

identified with the higher energy half-width of the absorption spectrum. To determine the highest or lowest energy components of the spectra, the energy at which the spectra falls to 5% of their peak value may be used, although the results are not very sensitive to this criterion [21].

2.3.2 Transition Rate

Deexcitation of upper energy levels can occur either radiatively, giving rise to spontaneous or stimulated emission, or nonradiatively through multiphonon relaxation processes. The probability of multiphonon decay depends on the energy separation of the involved levels and on the phonon energy of the host material.

In accordance with the Judd-Ofelt theory [12, 13], spontaneous radiative transition rates of all Er^{3+} excited state levels is determined by [23, 24]:

$$A(JJ') = \frac{64\pi^4 \nu^3}{3h(2J+1)}\left(\frac{n(n^2+2)^2}{9}S_{ed} + n^3 S_{md}\right) \tag{9}$$

where S_{ed} and S_{md} are the electric dipole and magnetic dipole line strengths respectively, n is the refractive index of the isotropic media and J is the energy level quantum number (energy level population). The total radiative transition rate of level J is:

$$A_T = \sum_{J'} A(JJ') \tag{10}$$

The radiative life time of level J can be obtained from the radiative transition rate as follows:

$$\tau_R(J) = \left[\sum_{J'} A(JJ')\right]^{-1} \tag{11}$$

The above equation is expressed as the sum of all lower energy levels J'.

The quantum efficiency of the radiative transition is defined as:

$$\eta = \frac{\tau_{meas}}{\tau_R} \tag{12}$$

where τ_{meas} is the measured fluorescence decay lifetime of level J and τ_R is the radiative life time . The nonradiative transition rate W_{nr} is defined as:

$$W_{nr} = \frac{1}{\tau_{meas}} - \frac{1}{\tau_R} \tag{13}$$

The measured lifetimes of Er3+ energy levels $^4I_{11/2}, ^4F_{9/2}, ^4S_{3/2}$ are far below the calculated radiative lifetime, which clearly shows the nonradiative transition mechanisms [11].

Nonradiative transition rates are mainly influenced by host materials. The nonradiative transition rate drops exponentially with the increase of the maximum phonon energy. Thus nonradiative relaxation is often dominant compared with the radiative process in a host material with higher phonon energy. Relative efficiency of the radiative and nonradiative relaxation determines the intensity distribution of fluorescence spectroscopy.

The nonradiative transition rate from one excited state to the adjacent lower level is estimated by the energy gap:

$$W_{nr} = B \exp(-\alpha \Delta E) \tag{14}$$

B and α are constants related to the host material, which are independent of the energy levels of Er3 + ions. ΔE is the energy gap between the excited state and the next lower energy level. Calculations show that except for level $^4I_{13/2}$, all levels of the relaxation process are mainly nonradiative decay. This is due to the large energy gap between $^4I_{13/2}$ and $^4I_{15/2}$ (6515cm^{-1}), while energy gaps of the other excited states are very small. According to the literature [23, 24], it shows that the nonradiative transition rate of the excited level to the next lower level is much larger than the radiative transition rate by about 3-7 orders of magnitude. Therefore, in the establishment of the rate equation model, it is reasonable to ignore the radiative transition from $^4S_{3/2}$ to $^4I_{15/2}$, $^4 F_{9/2}$ to $^4I_{15/2}$, $^2 H_{11/2}$ to $^4I_{15/2}$, etc.

2.4. Energy Transfer Processes of Er^{3+}

Many researchers have studied population quenching processes of Er^{3+}, which result from various ion-ion energy transfer processes that affect the population dynamics of Er^{3+}. These processes generally lead to additional nonradiative relaxation and decrease the overall luminescence efficiency. The effect of the ion-ion exchange processes becomes significant in high dopant concentrations where the distances between the dopant ions in the host are reduced and an energy exchange can occur between similar ions of the same dopant or different ions in co-doped materials. The following paragraphs describe several dominant energy transfer processes of Er^{3+}.

2.4.1. ESA - Excited State Absorption

Figure 3 depicts the excited state absorption processes of three different pump wavelengths. Ions at the excited state absorb pump photons or signal photons and move to a higher level after the transition, and the photon energy dissipates through heat or spontaneous emission even if there is a final return to the $^4I_{13/2}$ level. With the pump wavelength of 0.82 μm, one erbium ion is excited by one photon to the $^4I_{9/2}$ level and then is rapidly relaxed to the $^4I_{13/2}$ level by nonradiative multi-phonon emission. An Erbium ion in the metastable level can absorb a second photon of 0.82 μm and move to a higher level $^2H_{11/2}$. Ions on level $^2H_{11/2}$ rapidly decay to levels of $^4I_{13/2}$ by the ion-phonon emission. Thus the energy of the second photon is converted into heat. Therefore, two pump photons produce only one metastable state ion with the loss of one photon of energy. If during this process a high energy ion decays directly back to the ground state, two pump photons are both lost. The ESA process depends greatly on the pump intensity, and the

ESA transition rate increases with pump intensity. Thus, excited state absorption reduces the pumping efficiency.

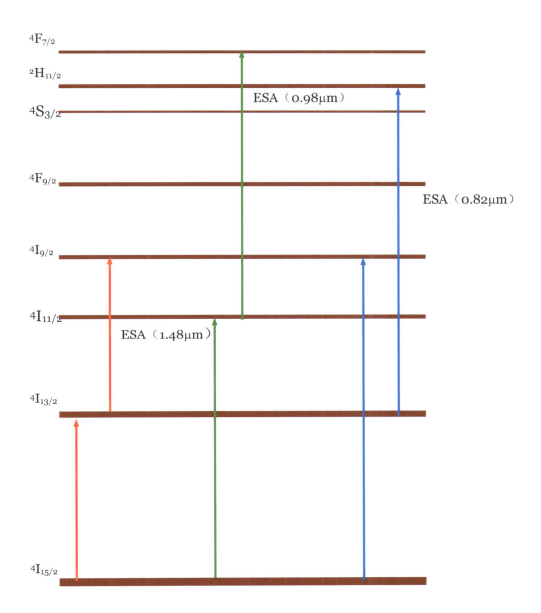

Figure 3. Schematic representation of excited state absorption

2.4.2. CUC - Cooperative Upconversion

With high erbium doping concentrations, interaction between the electric dipole moment of two erbium ions is affected by the small spacing between two erbium ions. As shown in Figure 4, due to the resonance between the energies, in the first excited state (level $^4I_{13/2}$), one ion may transfer energy to another ion and return to the ground state, and the ion which received the energy from the other ion is transferred to a higher energy level (level $^4I_{9/2}$). Ions at the higher energy level (level $^4I_{9/2}$) rapidly decay to the level $^4I_{13/2}$ through a multi-phonon emission, thus one photon energy at the first excited state (level $^4I_{13/2}$) is lost. Therefore, the number of erbium ions at the first excited state at a given pump rate is decreased. Cooperative upconversion (CUC) is affected mainly by the doping concentration and CUC becomes more significant with increasing doping concentration. CUC is also affected by the pump power, since cooperative conversion requires two ions in the excited state. Thus, at low pump levels CUC is not obvious, but it becomes more significant as the pump intensity increases.

With different doping methods of Er^{3+} ions, second order upconversion could be present as shown in Figure 4 [25]. First, two Er^{3+} ions in the $^4I_{13/2}$ state interact to yield an ion in the $^4I_{9/2}$ state, which is followed by a nonradiative relaxation to the $^4I_{11/2}$ level. Then, two ions in the $^4I_{11/2}$ level interact to yield an ion in the $^2H_{11/2}$ level, which relaxes to the $^4S_{3/2}$ level, which causes fluorescence at multiple wavelengths due to the upcoversion at the second excited state $^4I_{11/2}$. In particular, second-order upconversion is the leading detrimental effect of reducing the photon energy at the excited states at high erbium concentrations of $\geq 1 \times 10^{21}$ cm^{-3} [26].

2.4.3. CR - Cross-Relaxation

The cross-relaxation process is the reverse process of cooperative upconversion, as shown in Figure 4. Two ions in low and high-level energy states interact and transit upwardly and downwardly to the middle level. Cross relaxation between $^4I_{15/2}$ and $^4I_{9/2}$ levels contributes to the population inversion, and cross-relaxation between $^4I_{15/2}$ and $^4F_{7/2}$ levels can be ignored between of the limited number of particles on the $^4F_{7/2}$ level. Corresponding to the second-order upconversion process, second-order cross-relaxation is also present as shown in Fig. 4.

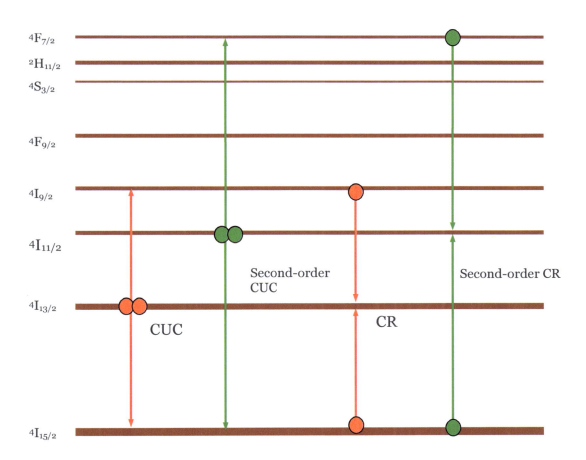

Figure 4. Schematic representation of cooperative upconversion and cross-Relaxation.

Chapter 3

Analysis of silicon waveguides with multiple erbium doped regions

3.1. Introduction

Silicon light emitters are the missing links for future silicon-based photonic integration. A main challenge is to find a way to attain high quantum efficiency [27]. Many approaches have been employed to obtain optical gain in silicon, ranging from silicon nanocrystals to erbium-doped silicon, and yet, there have been few achievements [28-31]. Conventionally, light amplification at telecommunication wavelengths has been achieved using erbium-doped low-index host materials, such as erbium-doped oxide glass (phosphosilicate and soda-lime glasses) and ceramic thin films (Al_2O_3, Y_2O_3) [32-34]. Well-developed fabrication processes and high erbium solubility in a small volume have attracted great interest in these host materials, and hence planar dielectric waveguides have been fabricated to deliver wafer scale light amplifiers. For instance, Al_2O_3: Er^{3+} waveguides with 0.1 dB/cm background loss have been fabricated with low-cost and reliable fabrication processes, 80nm gain bandwidth and up to 2.3dB/cm amplification performance [35, 36]. The net gain can be further enhanced to 4.1 dB/cm in similar waveguide devices using phosphate glass [37].

Silicon slot waveguides, sub-micrometer slots embedded between waveguides, have been experimentally demonstrated to provide a high optical confinement in the slot region that can accommodate possible optical gain mediums [38, 39]. Approaches that confine light in low-index structures have been presented to show achievements in CMOS-compatible light-emitting devices. To achieve lasing, gain provided by the active material in the slot region must be high enough to overcome loss in the whole waveguide. One way of achieving this goal is to use horizontal slot waveguides [40], slots sandwiched between amorphous silicon (α-silicon). However, a main advantage of using silicon comes with electronic integration. Thus, the use of crystalline silicon is important for enabling electronic integration.

In this chapter, we analyze the structure of crystalline silicon waveguides with multiple erbium doped Al_2O_3 regions sandwiched in between. The advantages of the proposed structures are: (1) Light amplification at telecommunication wavelengths is induced by erbium doped Al_2O_3. (2) Electronic tuning capabilities such as switching and modulating are provided by the crystalline silicon platform.

A theoretical study presented in this chapter evaluates the gain and loss competitions in multi-trench crystalline silicon waveguides with erbium-doped Al_2O_3. Especially, effects of erbium concentration, power confinement and nonlinear losses on gain are discussed in detail. Different power distribution profiles in the waveguides and erbium concentrations up to $5\times10^{20}cm^{-3}$ have been considered. In particular, nonlinear losses that mitigate the optical gain, including excited-state absorption and upconversion in erbium-doped Al_2O_3 and free carrier absorption in silicon have been analyzed. Different design geometries and the associated nonlinear losses have been discussed for their impacts on optical gain. Multi-trench geometries are shown to ultimately increase the power confinement in the low index regions and produce higher gain to nonlinear loss ratio. We show that net gain can be improved as much as 0.38dB/cm in multi-trench waveguides compared to single trench waveguides.

3.2. Device structures

The device structures of silicon rib waveguides with multiple erbium-doped Al_2O_3 regions used in this study are depicted in Figure 5. In these structures, the silicon (refractive index n_{si}=3.48) rib waveguide acts as a platform to hold rectangular low-index erbium-doped Al_2O_3 ($n_{Er-Al2O3}$ =1.64) regions. In particular, two groups of waveguide geometries (WG1 and WG2 of Figure 5) are investigated in detail to evaluate the effects of power distribution on nonlinear losses. Waveguide height was fixed at 0.8 μm and waveguide widths of 0.6 μm and 1 μm were selected for groups of WG1 and WG2, respectively. Selection of waveguide width was in accordance with the desired single-mode condition in both polarizations, as well as accommodating several low-index erbium-doped active regions [41]. Minimal trench widths and spacings between the trenches were designed as 0.1 μm owing to practical fabrication precision, complexity, and cost. As a result, maximum numbers of trenches were constrained for different waveguide width designs. Length of the waveguide was selected to be 1cm due to limitations of practical fabrication precision, complexity, and cost.

For WG1 in Figure 5(a), two subgroups, single trench (WG1A) and two trenches (WG1B) configurations were proposed and analyzed. For WG2 in Figure 5(b), two trenches (WG2A) and four trenches (WG2B) were proposed and analyzed. In the above-mentioned designs, a maximum of two trenches (WG1B) for WG1 were designed with a total active area of 0.2 μm ×0.7 μm and a maximum of four trenches (WG2B) for WG2 were designed with a total active area of 0.4 μm ×0.7 μm. For the same silicon waveguide dimensions (width and height), the total erbium-doped active area remained the same for different numbers of active regions (subgroup A or B), showing the effects of trench numbers. By using waveguides with different widths (WG1 and WG2), our goal was to demonstrate how the power distributions and loss mechanisms in the waveguides are affected.

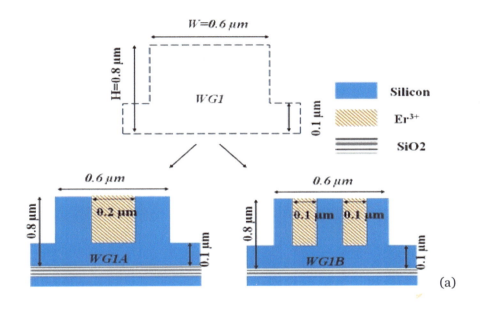

(a)

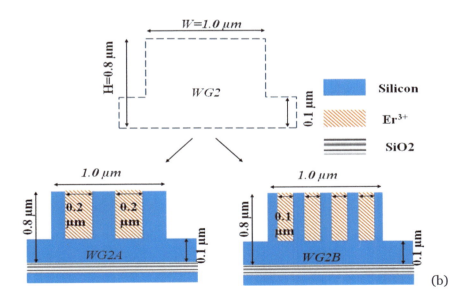

(b)

Figure 5. (a) Illustrations of WG1 of waveguide dimensions (0.6 μm width, 0.8 μm height, 0.1 μm trench

width), WG1A (Single trench) and WG1B (Two trenches), waveguide length=1cm.

(b) Illustrations of WG2 of waveguide dimensions (1 μm width, 0.8 μm height, 0.1 μm trench width),

WG2A (Two trenches) and WG2B (Four trenches), waveguide length=1cm.

3.3. Theoretical analysis

To evaluate signal amplification by erbium ions, power, signal and ASE profiles along the waveguide, population inversion and power confinement need to be analyzed. After determining signal and pump power distributions, signal evolution along the waveguide was performed by separating the signal propagation in silicon and in erbium-doped Al_2O_3. The theoretical model presented in this section included gain and loss mechanisms in erbium doped Al_2O_3 regions and silicon regions, as summarized in Figure 6. As silicon's absorption coefficient was found to be $\geq$ 100 cm^{-1} at shorter wavelengths, 1.48 μm of pumping was observed to be the only feasible wavelength considered in this model.

Prior to modeling, finite element analysis introduced in section 3.3.1 was performed on each waveguide geometry to obtain normalized power distribution. Then, analysis of pump, signal, and amplified spontaneous emissions (ASE) variation in erbium-doped Al_2O_3 was carried out based on four-level rate equations as discussed in section 3.3.2. In the silicon region, this model emphasizes free carrier induced nonlinear losses in section 3.3.3. After evaluating signal, pump, and ASE power in the waveguide at each propagation step, the total power was redistributed in the geometry. Finally, aggregate signal gains of the proposed structures were calculated based on the propagation equations discussed in section 3.3.4 at the end of the waveguide [42, 43].

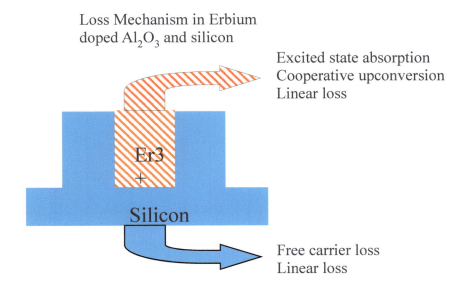

Loss Mechanism in Erbium doped Al_2O_3 and silicon

Excited state absorption
Cooperative upconversion
Linear loss

Er3+

Silicon

Free carrier loss
Linear loss

Figure 6. Gain and loss mechanisms in Erbium doped AL_2O_3 and silicon based on the theoretical model in the proposed structures.

3.3.1. Mode analysis of silicon waveguides with erbium doped Al_2O_3

When electromagnetic field equations are used to solve for the field distribution in the waveguides, for a given boundary condition, different discrete characteristic solutions may exist. Each particular solution is called a mode (or eigenfunction). In the same refractive index along the (z direction) regular waveguide, the optical field can be expressed as:

$$\begin{pmatrix} \vec{E} \\ \vec{H} \end{pmatrix}(x, y, z, t) = \begin{pmatrix} \vec{e} \\ \vec{h} \end{pmatrix}(x, y)e^{-i\beta z}e^{i\omega t} \qquad (15)$$

Optical field distribution in space can be expressed as

$$\begin{pmatrix} \vec{E} \\ \vec{H} \end{pmatrix}(x, y, z) = \begin{pmatrix} \vec{e} \\ \vec{h} \end{pmatrix}(x, y)e^{-i\beta z} \qquad (16)$$

where β is the propagation constant, and $\bar{e}(x,y)$ and $\bar{h}(x,y)$ are the mode field amplitudes.

The electromagnetic field solution $\bar{e}(x,y)$ and $\bar{h}(x,y)$ can be divided into guided wave modes and radiative modes. The intrinsic value of the radiative mode is in a range of continuous spectrum. Energy is radiated to the substrate and the cladding, thus decreasing the field amplitude. When the optical waveguide is excited with a light source, all the guided wave modes and radiative modes will be excited at the front end of the waveguide. The amplitude decrease of radiative modes can be ignored finally as propagating along the waveguide. Thus, we only consider the guided wave mode to form a steady-state mode distribution along the waveguide.

Maxwell's equations can be divided into two separate groups: (1) Ey, Hx, Hz, also called a transverse magnetic (TM) wave, where electric field is linearly polarized perpendicular to the substrate, and (2) Hy, Ex, Ez, also called a transverse electric (TE) wave, the electrical field is linearly polarized parallel to the substrate. The corresponding guided modes are TEm and TMm modes as shown in Figure 7. Often for a two-dimensional rectangular dielectric waveguide, there is no pure TEmn mode and no pure TMmn since both Ez and Hz exist at the same time.

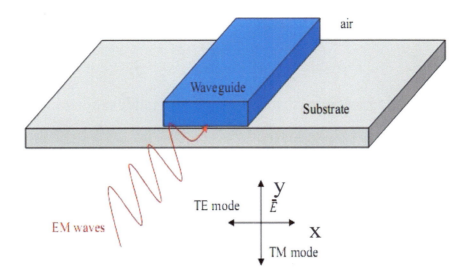

Figure 7. Orientation of coordinate axes of EM mode with respect to the substrate. When the electric field is parallel to the substrate, a TE mode is defined while if the electrical field is perpendicular to the substrate, a TM mode is defined.

For a limited number of ideal, simple waveguide configurations, modes and corresponding propagation constants can be found analytically. However, for a majority of realistic waveguides, numerical simulations are essential. Even the waveguides with relatively simple cross-sections and refractive index profiles in reality may suffer from anisotropy, inhomogeneities due to fabrication tolerances, and material losses that affect their modal properties. Depending on the refractive index profile and other waveguide characteristics, various types of modes may be supported, including antiguiding, leaky, lossy, or radiating modes.

Numerical analysis methods used in electromagnetic field analysis include finite element method, finite difference method, mode matching, transverse resonance method, etc. [44-47] . Because of its high accuracy and versatility, finite element method (FEM) is the most widely used with its more accurate numerical techniques and serves as the basis of various approximate calculations. Finite element method is particularly suitable for complex geometries and distribution of dielectric properties, can solve almost any broad cross-section and refractive index distribution of waveguide modes and field distribution of the media and has been successfully used to analyze any section of a straight waveguide. The finite element method (FEM) is used for finding the approximate solution of partial differential equations (PDE) that handle complex geometries (and boundaries), such as waveguides with arbitrary cross-sections, with relative ease. The field region is divided into elements of various shapes as shown in Figure 8, such as triangles and rectangles, allowing the use of an irregular grid. The solution approach is based either on eliminating the differential equation completely (steady state problems), or rendering the PDE into an equivalent ordinary differential equation, which is then solved using standard techniques, such as finite differences. In a context of optical waveguides, the FEM can be used for mode solving and propagation problems. Two approaches to solve waveguide problems include the variational method and the weighted residual (Galerkin) method. Both methods lead to the same eigenvalue equation that needs to be solved.

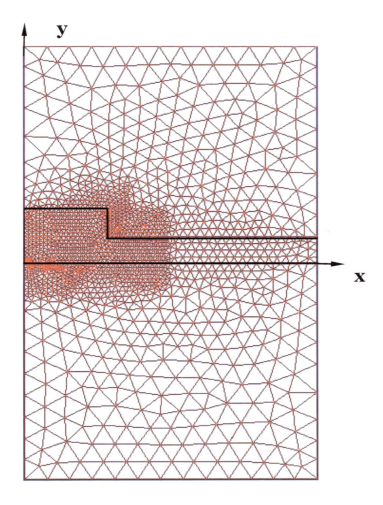

Figure 8. FEM mesh used for guiding mode of rib waveguide (only half of the waveguide is shown due to the symmetry)

3.3.2. Rate equations of Er³⁺

Energy level model of Er³⁺ with 1480 nm pumping scheme is presented in Figure 9, showing all possible transitions induced by the pump radiation.

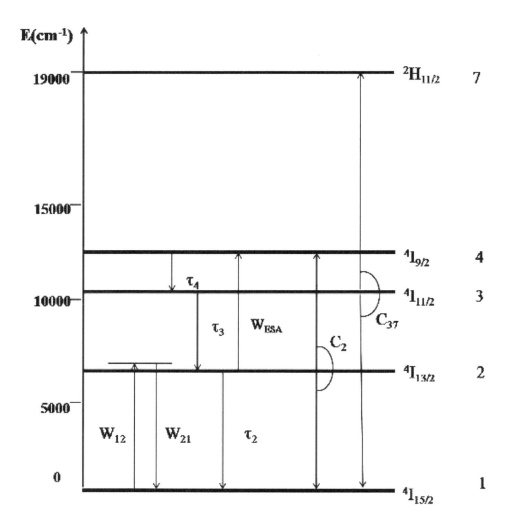

Figure 9 Energy levels for Er³⁺ pumping at 1.48 μm

The rate equations following the energy levels presented in Figure 9 can be expressed as [42, 48-50]:

$$\frac{dN_1}{dt} = -W_{12}N_1 - R_{12}N_1 + W_{21}N_2 + R_{21}N_2 + \frac{N_2}{\tau_2} + C_2 N_2^2 - C_{37} N_3^2 \qquad (18)$$

$$\frac{dN_2}{dt} = W_{12}N_1 + R_{12}N_1 - W_{21}N_2 - R_{21}N_2 - \frac{N_2}{\tau_2} + \frac{N_3}{\tau_3} - 2C_2 N_2^2 - W_{24}N_2 \qquad (19)$$

$$\frac{dN_3}{dt} = -\frac{N_3}{\tau_3} + \frac{N_4}{\tau_4} - C_{37}N_3{}^2 \qquad (20)$$

$$\frac{dN_4}{dt} = -\frac{N_4}{\tau_4} + C_2 N_2^2 + W_{24}N_{24} \qquad (21)$$

$$N_T = N_1 + N_2 + N_3 + N_4$$

$$R_{ij} = \frac{\sigma_{ij}(\nu_s)}{h\nu_s}I_s + \sum_{j=1}^{m}\frac{\sigma_{ij}(\nu_j)}{h\nu_j}[I_{ASE+} + I_{ASE-}] \qquad (22)$$

$$W_{ij} = \frac{\sigma_{ij}(\nu_P)}{h\nu_P}I_P \qquad (23)$$

Cooperative upconversion and exited-state absorption were taken into account in erbium-doped Al_2O_3 by these rate equations; N_T is the total erbium concentration; N_1, N_2, N_3, N_4 are the Er^{3+} concentrations in the energy levels $^4I_{15/2}$, $^4I_{13/2}$, $^4I_{11/2}$, and $^4I_{9/2}$, respectively, as shown in Figure 9; τ_2, τ_3, τ_4 are the luminescence lifetimes corresponding to each energy level, respectively; and C_2 is the cooperative upconversion coefficient. For high erbium concentrations, second-order upconversion was found to play a critical role, and hence, was included in this model (C_{37}). However, at low erbium concentrations ($\sim 3\times10^{20}\,cm^{-3}$), if the waveguide is carefully designed and fabricated, the effect of second-order upconversions is negligible and can be ignored ($C_{37}=0$) [26]. R_{12}, R_{21}, W_{12}, and W_{21} are induced signal and pump transition rates; W_{ESA} is the induced ESA rate; I_s, I_p, and $I_{ASE\pm}$ are the signal, pump, and amplified spontaneous emission intensities, respectively; and σ_{ij} is the emission or absorption cross-section.

3.3.3 Free carrier absorption in silicon

Electron and hole pairs in silicon are generated by TPA during the propagation, and those free carriers induce additional optical absorption. This process can be explained as follows: when the input photon energy is smaller than the bandgap of silicon crystal (1.1eV), the direct absorption is absent and TPA becomes dominant in loss. When two photons are absorbed through phonon assisted TPA process, it creates an electron-hole pair. The carriers also induce an absorption effect called free carrier absorption that further increases the attenuation, as shown in Figure 10. Free carriers generated by two-photon-absorption in silicon-on-insulator SOI waveguides can introduce large losses which limit the usable pump power for Raman amplification at telecommunication wavelengths[51].

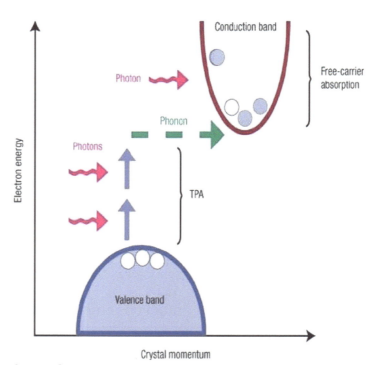

Figure 10. Two photon absorption and free carrier absorption in silicon (Figure courtesy: Jalali,2008 [51])

As light propagated along the waveguide, its pump intensity I(z) would suffer from different linear and nonlinear losses [52]:

34

$$\frac{dI(z)}{dz} = -(\alpha_{lin} + \alpha_{fca}(z))I(z) - \beta I^2(z) \tag{24}$$

where α_{lin} is the linear loss, $\alpha_{fca}(z)$ is the free carrier absorption, and β is the TPA coefficient. In the silicon waveguides, the linear loss is mainly due to scattering from rib wall roughness and does not contribute to any free-carrier generation because of the photons at pump wavelength do not have sufficient energy to excite any interband transitions. To calculate the contribution of free-carrier absorption to the loss, we first need to know the number of carriers generated from TPA inside the waveguide. The total optical power absorbed due to TPA along the waveguide may be described as [52]:

$$P_{tpa}(z) = \frac{\beta}{A_{eff}} \int_0^z P^2(z)dz \tag{25}$$

where A_{eff} is the nonlinear effective area defined as [52]:

$$A_{eff} = \frac{(\int\limits_{-\infty}^{\infty} \int\limits_{-\infty}^{\infty} |E(x,y)|^2 \, dxdy)^2}{(\int\limits_{-\infty}^{\infty} \int\limits_{-\infty}^{\infty} |E(x,y)|^4 \, dxdy)} \tag{26}$$

Where $E(x,y)$ is the mode-field profile of the waveguide, which can be calculated by simulation software.

An electron-hole pair (EHP) will be generated for every two photons (i.e., TPA) absorbed. The rate of EHP generation and recombination inside the waveguide is [52]:

$$\frac{dN_{eph}(z)}{dt} = \frac{P_{tpa}(z)}{2h\upsilon} - \frac{N_{ehp}(z)}{\tau_c} \tag{27}$$

Where $h\upsilon$ is the photon energy and τ_c is the carrier lifetime. The carrier lifetime in the waveguide is mainly characterized by EHP recombination time at both guiding layer (bulk re-combination) and Si/SiO₂ interface (surface recombination). Surface

35

recombination results in a quick diffusion of carriers towards the sample surface or Si/SiO2 interface, which results in a lowering of the measured lifetime compared to the bulk value. At steady state, $dN_{ehp}/dt=0$, thus number of EHP generated from TPA

$$N_{ehp(z)} = \frac{\tau_0 P_{tpa}(z)}{2h\upsilon} \qquad (28)$$

Carrier density calculation is nontrivial because of nonlinear effects such as carrier density dependent carrier lifetimes and mobilities. A simple estimate of carrier density may be made by assuming that the carriers are uniformly distributed inside the waveguide. Thus, the carrier density N(z) can be calculated from Eqs. (27) and (28):

$$N(z) = \frac{\tau_0 \beta \int_0^z P^2(z)dz}{2h\upsilon A_{wg} A_{eff} z} \qquad (29)$$

where A_{wg} is the physical dimension of waveguide area. Finally, free-carrier absorption coefficient α_{fca} can be described from the classical Drude model:

$$\alpha_{fca}(z) = \frac{q^3 \lambda^2}{4\pi^2 c^3 \varepsilon_0 n} \left(\frac{N_e(z)}{m^2_e \mu_e} + \frac{N_h(z)}{m^2_h \mu_h} \right) \qquad (30)$$

where $N_e(z)/N_h(z)$ is the free-carrier density, n is the refractive index of silicon, q is the electron charge, ε_0 is free-space permittivity, c is the light velocity in vacuum, m_e/m_h is the effective mass and m_e/m_h is the free-carrier mobility, subscripts e and h denote electrons and holes, respectively. Since the number of electrons and holes are created in equal numbers by TPA, $N_e(z)$ and $N_h(z)$ are equal to N(z) in Eq. (29).

In this section, a theoretical model of the free-carrier absorption which reduces the pump power in silicon waveguides with erbium doped Al_2O_3 is introduced. The modeling of free carrier effect in silicon is discussed as following. With regard to free carrier absorption in silicon, at each propagation step, $I_{Si}(x, y, z)$ represents the variation of pump intensity at each individual point <x, y, z> in silicon, and can be expressed based on equation (24) as:

$$\frac{dI_{Si}(x,y,z)}{dz} = -\alpha_{fca}(z)I_{Si}(x,y,z) - \beta I_{Si}^{2}(x,y,z)$$

(31)

Where

$$\alpha_{fca}(z) = 1.45 \times 10^{-17} \left(\frac{\lambda}{1.55}\right)^{2} N(x,y,z)$$ (cm^{-1})

(32)

β represents the TPA coefficient and α_{fca} (z) represents the free carrier absorption expressed in [53]. Also, N (x, y, z) is the free carrier density at each individual point in silicon and it is deduced from equation (29):

$$N(x,y,z) = \frac{\tau_{0}\beta I_{Si}^{2}(x,y,z)}{2hv} + f(i)$$

(33)

where τ_0 is the free carrier recombination life time. The last term f(i) is the free carrier absorption induced by current injection in the event of electronic modulation. Since electronic manipulation is not discussed in this paper, free carrier absorption induced by carrier injection is ignored in the following numerical calculations. At each propagation step, pump power in silicon affected by free carrier absorption can be represented as:

$$P_{si}(z) = \iint_{Si} I_{si}(x,y,z)dxdy$$

(34)

Upon determination of the pump profile along the waveguide, free carrier losses of the pump can be estimated as:

$\Delta P_{si} = P_{si}(z+1) - P_{si}(z)$

(35)

3.3.4 Propagation equations

The steady-state evolution of pump, signal, and amplified spontaneous emission powers in erbium-doped Al_2O_3 are expressed as propagation equations [50]:

$$\frac{dP_p(z)}{dz} = -\gamma_p(z)P_p(z) - \alpha_p P_p(z) \tag{36}$$

$$\frac{dP_s(z)}{dz} = [\gamma_{21}(z,\nu_s) - \gamma_{12}(z,\nu_s)]P_s(z,\nu_s) - \alpha_s P_s(z) \tag{37}$$

$$\frac{dP_{ASE+}(z,\nu_j)}{dz} = [\gamma_{21}(z,\nu_j) - \gamma_{12}(z,\nu_j)]P_{ASE+}(z,\nu_j) + Mh\nu_j\Delta\nu_j\gamma_{21}(z,\nu_j) - \alpha_s P_{ASE+}(z,\nu_j) \tag{38}$$

$$\frac{dP_{ASE-}(z,\nu_j)}{dz} = -[\gamma_{21}(z,\nu_j) - \gamma_{12}(z,\nu_j)]P_{ASE+}(z,\nu_j) - Mh\nu_j\Delta\nu_j\gamma_{21}(z,\nu_j) + \alpha_s P_{ASE+}(z,\nu_j) \tag{39}$$

Here the solution is obtained for boundary values of:

$P_p(0)=P_p$, $P_s(0)=P_s$, $P_{ASE+}(0, \upsilon_j)= P_{ASE-}(L, \upsilon_j)=0$ (j=1,2,...,m), where m is the number of frequency slots for amplified spontaneous emission. The coefficient M in equations (38) and (39) represents the number of guided modes at the signal wavelength. The absorption and emission coefficients $\gamma_{12}(z,\upsilon_s)$, $\gamma_{21}(z,\upsilon_s)$, and $\gamma_p(z)$ are given by

$$\gamma_{12}(z,\nu_s) = \iint_A \psi_s(x,y)\sigma_{12}(\nu_s)N_1(x,y,z)dxdy \tag{40}$$

$$\gamma_{21}(z,\nu_s) = \iint_A \psi_s(x,y)\sigma_{21}(\nu_s)N_2(x,y,z)dxdy \tag{41}$$

$$\gamma_p(z) = \iint_A \psi_p(x,y)[\sigma_{12}(\nu_p)N_1(x,y,z) - \sigma_{21}(\nu_p)N_2(x,y,z) + \sigma_{24}(\nu_p)N_2(x,y,z)]dxdy \tag{42}$$

where $\gamma_p(x,y)$ and $\gamma_s(x,y)$ are normalized pump and signal intensity profiles in the erbium doped regions, respectively. $\Psi_s(x,y)$ and $\Psi_p(x,y)$ are the normalized signal and pump intensity profile. A is the cross-sectional area of the erbium doped active region, and σ_{12}, σ_{21} and σ_{24} are the absorption and emission cross-sections.

3.3.5 Model Parameters

Spectroscopic and waveguide characteristics of the analyzed structures used in rate and propagation equations have to be determined experimentally to allow for a quantitative analysis of the optical amplification process. Therefore, the physical parameters used for Er^{3+} such as absorption and emission cross-sections, lifetimes and concentrations are from the experimental data shown in Table 1. In addition, the the physical parameters for the waveguide such as waveguide length and refractive index are also shown in Table 1.

Table 1. Physical parameters used for numerical analysis of silicon waveguide with erbium doped active regions [26, 48, 50]

Parameter	Value

Waveguide length	1cm
Pump wavelength	1.48μm
Signal power	1 μW
Er concentration (N_{Er})	5×10^{19}-5×10^{20}cm^{-3}
Pump absorption cross-section (1.48μm) σ_{12}	2.7×10^{-21}cm^2
Pump emission cross-section (1.48μm) σ_{21}	0.77×10^{-21}cm^2
Signal absorption cross-section (1.53μm) σ_{12}	5.8×10^{-21}cm^2
Signal emission cross-section (1.53μm) σ_{21}	6.1×10^{-21}cm^2
Excited state absorption cross-section (1.48μm) σ_{24}	0.85×10^{-21}cm^2
Cooperative upconversion C_2	$(2.65\times N_{Er}/10^{20}+3.38)\times10^{-18}$ cm^3/s
Second-order cooperative upconversion C_{37}	$(1\times10^{-17}$~$1\times10^{-15})$ cm^3/s
$^4I_{13/2}$ state lifetime τ_2	7.8ms
$^4I_{11/2}$ state lifetime τ_3	30μs
$^4I_{9/2}$ state lifetime τ_4	1ns
Refractive index of erbium doped active regions	1.64
Refractive index of silicon waveguide	3.48

3.4. Simulation results

The computer simulations presented in this section are based on the five-level analytical model introduced in section 3.3.2. This model requires solving a coupled system of rate and propagation equations, which comprises nonlinear and first-order differential equations that can be handled only numerically. For the practical implementation the MATLAB 7.0 program environment was used. This model assumes a 1480nm pumping scheme and takes into account the influence of co-operative up-conversion and excited state absorption processes as well as the amplified spontaneous emission in the signal wavelength region. Due to backward propagating ASE an iterative solution involving forward and backward integration of propagation equations must be employed.

Procedures of numerical simulations are summarized as follows:

(1) The normalized pump and signal intensity profiles, $\Psi_p(x,y)$, $\Psi_s(x,y)$, for fundamental TE mode are calculated in erbium-doped Al_2O_3 using finite element method by COMSOL multiphysics, maintaining the intensity distributions for both signal and amplified spontaneous emissions. Here, TE polarization is defined as the one in which the electric field vector is parallel to the waveguide slab.

(2) At each step in the propagation direction, by solving equations (18)–(21), Er^{3+} populations at energy levels N_1–N_4 at each point in the erbium region are calculated.

(3) Absorption and emission coefficient $\gamma_{12}(z,\upsilon_s)$, $\gamma_{21}(z,\upsilon_s)$, and $\gamma_p(z)$ are calculated using equations (40)–(42), through $\psi_p(x,y)$, $\psi_s(x,y)$, and N_1, N_2.

(4) Numerical integration of propagation equations (36)–(37) is achieved by Runge–Kutta based iterative procedure to obtain $P_p(z)$ and $P_s(z)$ at each step.

(5) The total pump power is then further attenuated by the nonlinear pump power loss in silicon (ΔP_{si}) at each propagation step as calculated using equation (35).

The above numerical modeling calculates signal gain as a function of pump power. Further, the numerical simulation evaluates the effects of mode field distribution, Er^{3+} concentrations, detrimental upconversion, excited state absorption and free carrier absorption as well as amplified spontaneous emission. Thus, parameters and characteristics of the proposed structures can be optimized to achieve the best possible performance.

3.4.1. Effects of power confinement & population inversion

As net gain and nonlinear losses are highly influenced by the optical intensity distribution, the impact of intensity distribution facilitated by different geometries (number of trenches) on each loss mechanism needs to be studied to determine the optical gain. The mode distributions in trenched waveguides are calculated using finite element method provided by COMSOL multiphysics. From these simulations, the confinement factor and the distribution of normalized power intensity in erbium-doped Al_2O_3 regions are extracted for the fundamental TE mode, as illustrated in Fig. 11(a) and (b), respectively. In this structure, TE polarization is characterized as the one in which the electric field vector is perpendicular to the trenches to provide high power confinement in the Er^{3+} regions. To have a fair comparison, the total volume of the Er^{3+} doped active regions is set to be equal for the same waveguide group (same waveguide width).

WG1 group	WG1A	WG1B
Power confinement in erbium doped Al_2O_3	16.04%	27.52%
WG2 group	WG2A	WG2B
Power confinement in erbium doped Al_2O_3	22.82%	33.85%

(a)

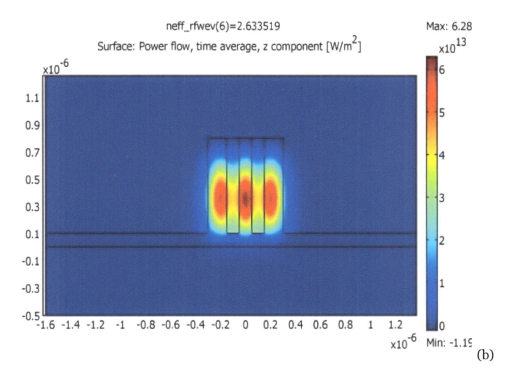

Figure 11 (a) Power Confinement factors of different proposed geometries.

(b) Illustration of normalized power intensity profile (/m²) of a two trenched waveguide (WG1B) in WG1 group.

In the analyzed devices, the degree of Er^{3+} population inversion in the slot regions is plotted along the length of the waveguide as shown in Figure 12. The population inversion of Er^{3+} is integrated over the thickness of the waveguide. The dip in the center of the waveguide is due to excited state absorption (ESA). The effect of ESA does not decrease over the length of the waveguide since linear loss in the waveguide is not considered. If linear waveguide loss is considered, the effect of ESA decreases along the length of the waveguide as a result of absorption by Er^{3+} and waveguide losses resulting in little or no dip at the end of the waveguide [54].

Degree of population inversion

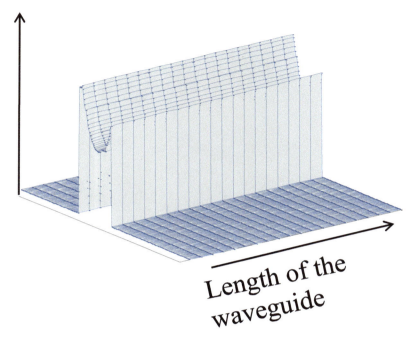

Length of the waveguide

Figure 12. Degree of inversion along the length of the waveguide. Calculations are made for WG1B, pumped at 100 mW at 1.48 μm (waveguide length=1cm).

3.4.2. Effects of 2nd order upconversion & Er^{3+} concentration

Second-order upconversion is known to cause fluorescence at multiple wavelengths, such as 520 nm green emission due to transitions from $^2H_{11/2}$ state to ground state, along with fluorescence at 545 nm, 660 nm and 850 nm [26, 48, 55, 56]. In particular, second-order upconversion is the leading detrimental effect at high erbium concentrations of $\geq 1 \times 10^{21}\,cm^{-3}$ [48]. A theoretical estimate of the effects of the second-order upconversion has been performed by varying the second-order upconversion coefficient C_{37} based on the reported value [26] in equations (18)–(21). As the intensity distribution in the waveguide is nonuniform and the effect of C_{37} is intensity-dependent, population inversions are calculated at different geometrical locations (points A–I in Fig. 13a) in the erbium-doped Al_2O_3 region. Here, each point corresponds to different pump intensities as indicated by the contour lines in Fig. 13a. By using $C_{37} = 8 \times 10^{-16} cm^3/s$ [26], we have shown that population inversions decrease by at least 30% as depicted in Fig. 13b. Furthermore, second-order upconversion may not lead to overall net population inversion depending on the intensity distributions in the geometry, as indicated in Fig. 13b and in [25, 26, 49].

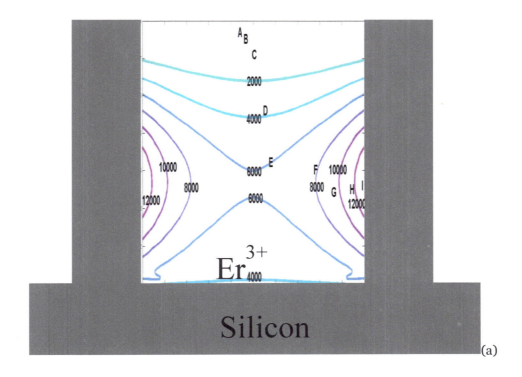

(a)

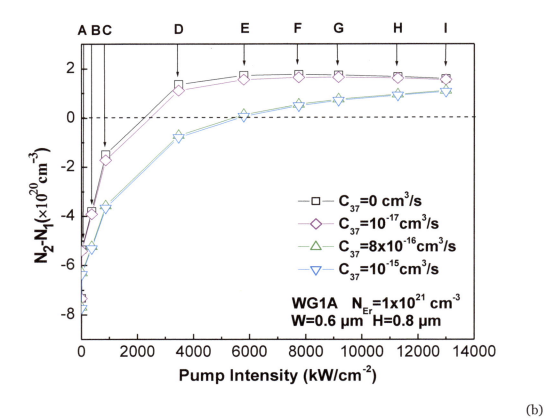

(b)

Fig 13 (a) Contour plot of pump intensity distribution within erbium doped Al_2O_3. Intensity distributions at exemplary points A-I show the estimated population inversion at locations with different pump intensities. Numbers on the contour lines represent intensity (kw/cm-3) (e.g. 2000 represents 2000 kw/cm-3).

(b) Population inversion calculated at points A-I with respect to different pump intensities and different values of C_{37}.

Although high erbium solubility in Al_2O_3 up to 3×10^{21} Er/cm3 is achievable, steady-state erbium population contributing to signal amplifications is greatly reduced by the second-order upconversion. Thus, high erbium concentration (e.g. $\geq1\times10^{21}$ Er/cm3) is not suitable for this analysis [25, 56]. High-order emission peaks are strongly reduced at low erbium concentration of $\leq5\times10^{20}$ Er/cm3, thus second-order upconversion can be neglected if the device is strategically fabricated and engineered [25, 49]. Subsequently, excited-state absorption and upconversion (excluding second-order upconversion) are the detrimental effects, which need to be incorporated at lower concentrations. Optimum erbium concentration of 5×10^{20} Er/cm3 is used in the following analysis to provide high optical gain as depicted in Figure 14, without second-order upconversion degradation.

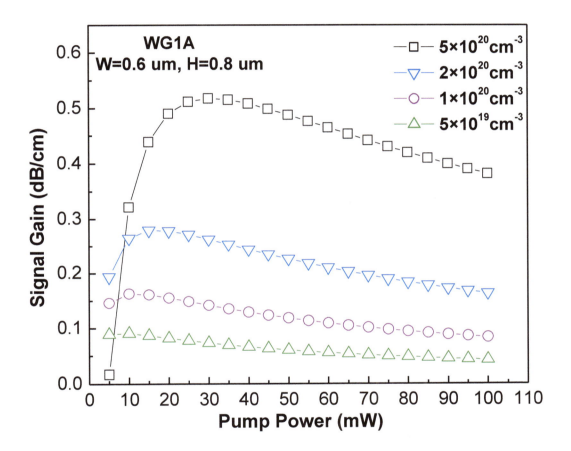

Figure 14. Signal gains of WG1A versus pump powers of different erbium doping concentrations (5×10^{20} cm-3, 2×10^{20} cm-3 , 1×10^{20} cm-3, 5×10^{19} cm-3) ,waveguide length=1cm).

3.4.3. Excited state absorption and cooperative upconversion

Although there have not been direct measurements of excited state absorption (ESA) in erbium-doped Al_2O_3 with 1.48μm pump wavelength, the ESA process from $^4I_{13/2}$ to $^4I_{9/2}$ is taken into account based on the experimental results for the gain calculation of erbium-doped planar waveguides and erbium-doped fiber amplifiers [25, 49, 56-58]. The ESA process is observed at lower erbium concentrations and explained as a phonon-assisted process [25]. Thus, the ESA cross-section determined from the experimental data is host-material dependent and nearly a factor of 10 smaller than the absorption cross-section for excitation of the first excited state [25].

In this section, by using the physical parameters determined experimentally [25, 58], ESA is found to deplete the optical gain at high pump intensities, especially at 1.48 μm pump wavelength. As illustrated in Figure 15, ESA is the strongest effect that reduces the gain at pump powers above 20 mW. Similarly, the cooperative upconversion process is affected by pump intensity at higher erbium concentration, and gain saturation is introduced at low pump power values, as shown in Figure 15. The gain profile generated by single-trench (WG1A) and double-trench (WG1B) waveguides are shown in Figure 16(a). These results indicate that device performance will be limited to low pump operations due to nonlinear losses in erbium-doped regions. Up to 0.38 dB/cm more signal gain is provided in the double-trench configuration when compared with the single-trench design, as shown in Figure 16(a).

Since linear loss is not considered in this analysis, nonlinear losses in the structures are calculated as:

$$L_{NF} = G_{sat} - G \tag{43}$$

Where G_{sat} is the saturation gain without linear and nonlinear losses and G is net optical gain considering nonlinear losses.

Where the saturation gain G_{sat} is estimated as:

$$G_{sat} = 4.43 \times (\sigma_{21}N_2 - \sigma_{12}N_1)\Gamma L \tag{44}$$

σ_{12} and σ_{21} are the Er^{3+} absorption and emission cross-sections, Γ is the power confinement factor and L is the waveguide length.

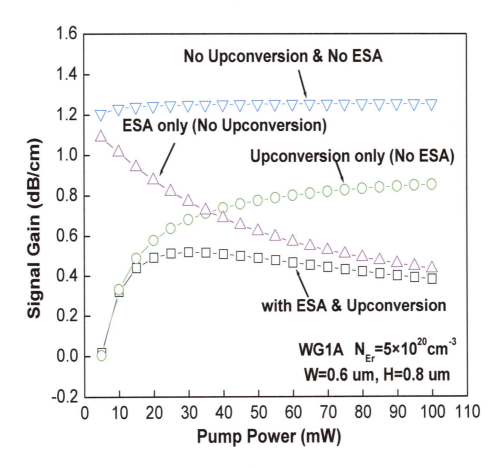

Figure 15. Signal gains of WG1A when no excited state absorption (ESA)and upconversion (UC), no UC, no ESA and with both ESA and UC respectively (waveguide length=1cm).

As shown in Figure 16 (a), nonlinear losses are increased in the double-trench structures. It is mainly caused by the non-uniformity of the power intensity profile in the multi-trench structures. The improved signal gain of the double-trench waveguide is mainly due to the improved power confinement factor thus improving the saturated gain without linear and nonlinear losses. Larger waveguides can accommodate more erbium-doped regions and have higher power confinement, as presented in Figure 11(a). Maximum achievable signal gain is improved in the larger waveguide dimensions by at least 0.3 dB/cm, comparing the four trenches configuration (WG2B) in Figure 16(b), with the two trenches configuration (WG1B) in Figure 16(a). With no linear loss in the system, as shown in Figure 16(b), the four-trench design can achieve the maximum gain of 1.1 dB/cm.

Linear loss due to scattering losses on the slots sidewalls is another parameter that should be considered. However, since linear loss is strictly a fabrication dependent parameter it is intentionally left out in this analysis. In the presence of linear loss, the effect of ESA decreases along the length of the waveguide as a result of absorption by Er^{3+} and waveguide losses. In addition, net gain may deplete or vanish depending on the magnitude of the linear loss.

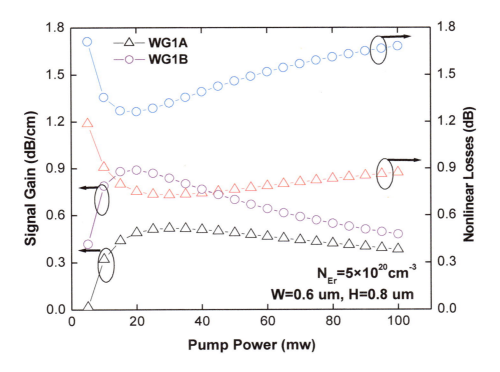

(a)

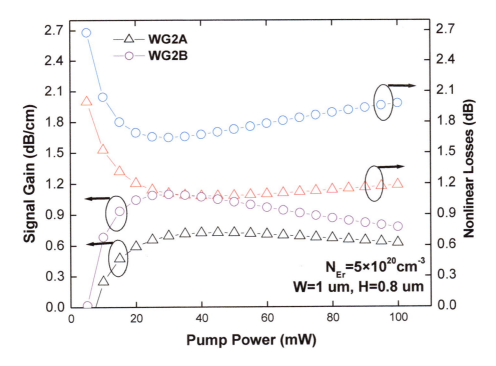

(b)

51

Figure 16 (a) Signal Gain and nonlinear losses versus pump power for WG1A and WG1B

(waveguide length=1cm).

(b) Signal Gain and nonlinear losses versus pump power for WG2A and WG2B

(waveguide length=1cm).

3.4.4. Noise Figure

The noise figure of the analyzed devices can be easily obtained once the amplified spontaneous emission has been spectrally resolved. By considering only signal-spontaneous emission beat noise, the noise figure can be expressed as[59] :

$$NF(dB) = 10\log_{10}[\frac{1}{G(z)} + \frac{P_{ASE+}(z,v_s)}{G(z)hv_s\delta v}]$$
(45)

G(z) is the signal gain, v_s is the signal frequency and δv is the width of the frequency slot used to compute $P_{ASE+}(z,v_s)$. In this study, the range of ASE spectrum calculated is 1.45μm∼1.65μm and $\delta v = 128$GHz as shown as shown in Figure 17.

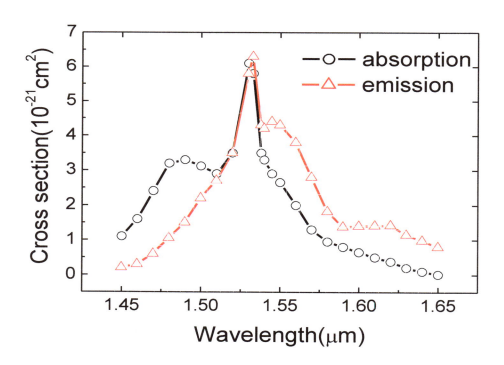

Figure 17. Emission and absorption cross-section spectrum and the frequency slot used to compute noise [14].

The noise figure analysis only applies to the unsaturated gain regime and evaluates the performance of the integrated amplifiers. Due to the non-uniformity of the pump profile, SNR is degraded in the multi-trench waveguide as shown in Figure 18. The multi-trench waveguide has higher power confinement and population inversion that leads to more spontaneous decay.

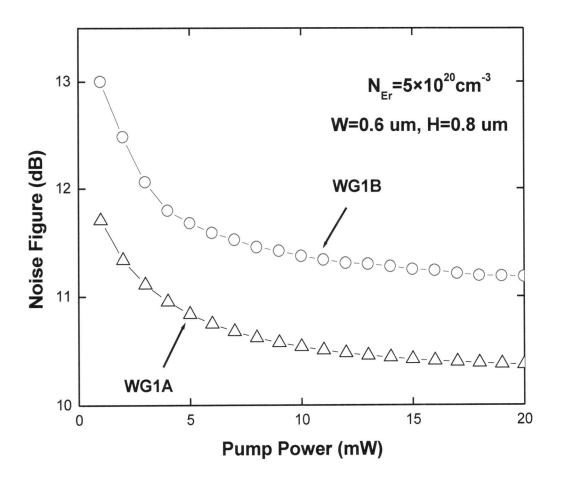

Figure 18. Noise figure versus input pump power for WG1B and WG1A (waveguide length=1cm).

3.4.5. Effects of free carrier absorption

At high pump powers, optical loss induced by free carrier absorption in silicon cannot be neglected [52]. As the maximum pump power in the proposed waveguide structures are limited by the ESA and upconversion, we expect to have limited free carrier losses in the silicon region. For pump power lower than 100 mW (to minimize ESA and upconversion effects), signal gain tends to decrease up to 3×10^{-4}dB/cm, as shown in Figure 19. These results indicate that the effect of the free carrier loss is negligible for pump powers less than 100 mW.

In addition, photon absorption in silicon due to the emissions from N_3 and N_4 states in the erbium doped Al_2O_3 regions is also considered. The upper state emissions disappear immediately in silicon nearby and may become the free carriers, because the absorption coefficient of Si layer is large, about 1000 cm^{-1}. Given the erbium ion population in N_3 and N_4 state (approximately 10^{18}cm^{-3}), lifetime of N_3 and N_4 states (approximately in the order of hundreds of μs) and the electron-hole recombination time (approximately in the order of ns), and the generated free carrier density is estimated to be approximately 10^{10}/cm^3 and thus it is negligible.

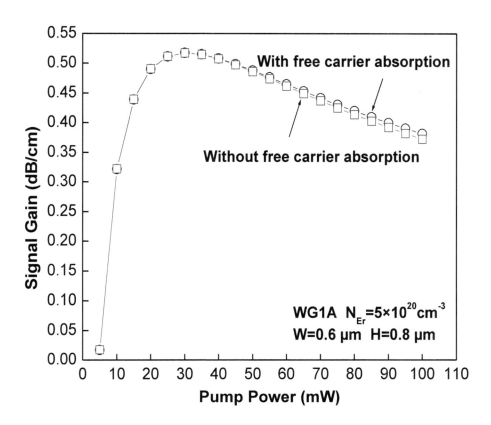

Figure 19. Signal gain vs. pump power for WG1A with and without free carrier absorption in silicon (waveguide length=1cm).

3.5. Summary

In summary, the effects of design geometries and nonlinear losses on gain in silicon waveguides with erbium-doped Al_2O_3 regions were studied. The performance of silicon waveguides with erbium-doped Al_2O_3 regions was limited by the upconversion and ESA. Second-order upconversion was found to be one of the detrimental effects that prevent signal gain at high erbium concentrations. Distributing erbium ions over multitrench areas improves higher gain to nonlinear loss ratio. Thus, 0.38 dB/cm higher signal amplification was generated when compared with a single-trench configuration.

Linear losses of the analyzed devices are mainly due to the fabrication processes. However, linear losses cannot be ignored in final designs and thus the fabrication processes need to be improved to provide ultimate high signal amplification.

Chapter 4

Erbium-Based Plasmonic-Assisted Vertical Emitter

4.1 Introduction

The use of plasmonics mixed with active photonic materials has been found to be promising due to the fact that the gain experienced through the emission of a gain medium is capable of counteracting the high attenuation of the electromagnetic wave. Also, net gain has been shown to be possible over macroscopic distances in a dielectric–metal–dielectric plasmonic waveguide, where the gain has been provided by an optically pumped layer of fluorescent conjugated polymer (known to have very large emission cross sections) adjacent to the metal surface [60]. A direct measurement of gain in propagating plasmons, using the long-range surface-plasmon–polariton supported by a symmetric metal stripe waveguide that incorporates optically pumped dye molecules in solution as the gain medium, has also been shown [61]. Similarly, experimental evidence of stimulated emission of surface plasmon-polaritons at telecom wavelengths (1532 nm) with erbium doped phosphate glass as a gain medium has been reported [62]. Room-temperature pulsed laser emission from optically pumped metallo-dielectric cavities has also been shown [63]. Additionally, lasing in metal-insulator-metal waveguides filled with electrically pumped semiconductor cores has been reported [64].

In this chapter, we propose a dielectric vertical emitter consisting of an erbium doped active material layer sandwiched between two metallic layers. In this work we use the metal layers for two purposes: (i) Guide the plasmonic pump mode (mainly confined in the erbium layer) that has the role of exciting the active material; and (ii) Act as mirrors in the vertical z direction to form a cavity resonating at 1532 nm. We employ the transverse resonance method [6] to compute the modes in the structure, and we focus on even (with respect to the x polarized electric field) TM modes. We show that such structures can be promising candidates for dielectric based vertical emitters.

4.2 Device structures

The proposed structure to achieve vertical emission at 1532 nm is illustrated in Figure 20. The structure is assumed to be infinitely extended in the xy plane. It is a multi-layered structure made of two semi-infinite layers with refractive index n_u and n_b (for simplicity, here assumed to be $n_u = n_b = 1$, or free space), two lossy metal layers of thickness d_m with refractive index n_m, and an active material doped layer (here assumed to be erbium doped alumina) with thickness d_g and refractive index n_g (equal to 1.6 in the absence of pumping).

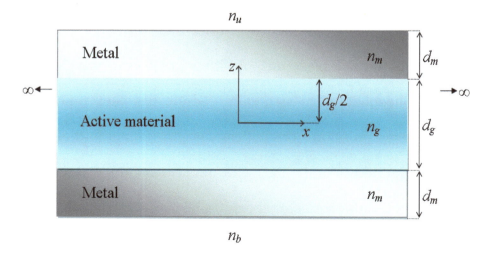

Figure 20. Lateral view of the proposed structure.

4.3 Theoretical analysis

4.3.1 Model of Er³⁺ doped Al₂O₃

The erbium doped Al_2O_3 layer is modeled as a simple three level system [65], where the pump wavelength is at 521 nm and the emission wavelength is at 1532 nm.

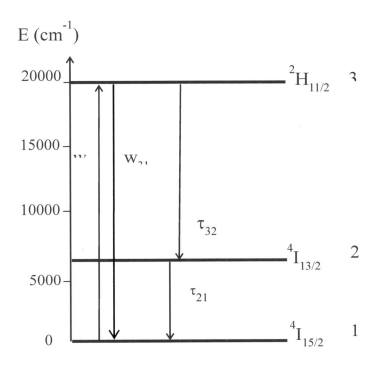

Figure 21, Three level model for Er³⁺ pumping at 0.54 μm

In the following equations (46-52), N_t is the total erbium concentration, and N_1, N_2, and N_3 are the Er³⁺ concentrations in the energy levels ⁴I₁₅/₂, ⁴I₁₃/₂, and ²H₁₁/₂, respectively [14]. The ⁴I₁₃/₂ state lifetime is τ_{21} and the decay time from ²H₁₁/₂ to ⁴I₁₃/₂ is τ_{32}. W_{13} and W_{31} are induced pump transition rates.

$$\frac{dN_1}{dt} = -W_{13}N_1 + W_{31}N_3 + \frac{N_2}{\tau_{21}} \qquad (46)$$

$$\frac{dN_2}{dt} = \frac{N_3}{\tau_{32}} - \frac{N_2}{\tau_{21}} \qquad (47)$$

$$\frac{dN_3}{dt} = W_{13}N_1 - W_{31}N_3 - \frac{N_3}{\tau_{32}}$$

(48)

Only a percentage Γ (approximately 90%) of Er^{3+} ions is estimated to reach level $^4I_{13/2}$ from level $^2H_{11/2}$ due to weak emission intensity at intermediate levels [66].

$$\frac{dN_2}{dt} = \frac{\Gamma \times N_3}{\tau_{32}} - \frac{N_2}{\tau_{21}}$$

(49)

The steady state Er^{3+} concentrations at each energy level can be calculated based on equations (42)-(44):

$$N_1 = \frac{W_{31} + (0.9/\tau_{32})}{W_{13}} \times N_3$$

(50)

$$N_2 = \frac{0.9 \times \tau_{21}}{\tau_{32}} \times N_3$$

(51)

$$N_3 = \frac{N_t}{\frac{W_{31} + (0.9/\tau_{32})}{W_{13}} + \frac{0.9 \times \tau_{21}}{\tau_{32}} + 1}$$

(52)

The induced pump transition rates can be expressed as [65]:

$$W_{ji} = \frac{g_i}{g_j} W_{ij} = \frac{3 \times \gamma_{rad,ji} \times \varepsilon \times |E_{ij}|^2 \lambda_{ji}^3}{8 \times \pi^2 \times \hbar \times \Delta\omega_{a,ij} \times \{1 + [2(\omega - \omega_a)/\Delta\omega_{a,ij}]^2\}}$$

(53)

In this model, W_{13} and W_{31} are equal, assuming no degeneracy. Since $\omega = \omega_a$ at the pump wavelength, the pump transition rate can be expressed as:

$$W_{31} = \frac{3 \times \gamma_{rad} \times \varepsilon \times |E|^2 \lambda^3}{8 \times \pi^2 \times \hbar \times \Delta\omega_a}$$

(54)

Where λ=521 nm at the pump wavelength, ε is the real part of the permittivity, $\Delta\omega_a$ is the bandwidth of the Lorentzian line shape (22.1Thz), γ_{rad} is the radiative transition rate. γ_{rad} can be expressed as [21]:

$$\gamma_{rad} = \frac{1}{\tau} = \frac{8\pi n^2}{c^2} \int_c \nu^2 \sigma_e(\nu) d\nu \tag{55}$$

Where τ is the radiative lifetime, n is the refractive index of the glass substrate, c is the velocity of light, and C denotes the spectral interval in which the Er^{3+} emission occurs. The shape of the emission and absorption cross sections with respect to frequency is assumed to be homogeneously broadened, and Lorentzian.

Table 2. Physical parameters used for Er^{3+} doped Al_2O_3 [14]

Parameter	Value
Pump wavelength	1.48μm
Er concentration (N_{Er})	$5\times10^{20}cm^{-3}$
Pump absorption cross-section (0.54μm) σ_{13}	$27.6\times10^{-21}cm^2$
Signal emission cross-section (1.53μm) σ_{21}	$5.7\times10^{-21}cm^2$
Pump absorption linewidth	20nm
Pump absorption linewidth	40nm
$^4I_{13/2}$ state lifetime τ_{21}	7.8ms
$^4I_{11/2}$ state lifetime τ_{33}	37μs

To determine the dielectric constant of Er^{3+} doped Al_2O_3, we calculated the complex refractive index. The dielectric constant used in Maxwell's equations is simply the square of the complex refractive index in a non-magnetic medium. From the absorption cross sections of Er^{3+}, we retrieve the imaginary part of the refractive index n_g in the presence of pumping, and then we apply Kramers-Kronig relations to compute the variation of the real part of the refractive index to have a causal and physical system.

The complex refractive index of the gain material Er^{3+} doped Al_2O_3 can be expressed as:

$$n_g(\omega) = n(\omega) + ik(\omega) \tag{56}$$

The imaginary part of the complex refractive index $k(\omega)$ can be computed from the gain obtained from Er^{3+} doped Al_2O_3 as described below:

The electric susceptibility can be expressed as:

$$X(\omega) = X'(\omega) + iX''(\omega) \tag{57}$$

The relationship of electric susceptibility and refractive index can be expressed:

$$n_g(\omega) = n(\omega) + ik(\omega) = \sqrt{1 + X'(\omega) + iX''(\omega)} \tag{58}$$

Using the approximation:

$$\sqrt{1 + X'(\omega) + iX''(\omega)} \approx 1 + \frac{X'(\omega)}{2} + i\frac{X''(\omega)}{2}, \tag{59}$$

The real and imaginary part of the refractive index can be expressed as:

$$n(\omega) \approx 1 + \frac{X'(\omega)}{2} \tag{60}$$

$$k(\omega) \approx \frac{X''(\omega)}{2} \tag{61}$$

The attenuation α of the electromagnetic wave can be expressed as:

$$\alpha \approx \frac{\omega}{c}X''(\omega) \tag{62}$$

Thus, the imaginary part of the refractive index can be related to the attenuation or absorption as:

$$k(\omega) \approx \frac{\alpha c}{2\omega} \tag{63}$$

The gain of Er^{3+} doped Al_2O_3 can be calculated as

$$G = e^{\Delta N \sigma l} \tag{64}$$

Where l is the length, ΔN is the population inversion and σ is the absorption cross section.

The gain of Er^{3+} doped Al_2O_3 can also be related to the electric field as:

$$G = |P_{out}/P_{in}| = |E_{out}/E_{in}|^2 \tag{65}$$

Thus,

$$|E_{out}| = |E_{in}| e^{-\Delta N \sigma l/2} = |E_{in}| e^{\alpha l} \tag{66}$$

Where $\alpha = -\Delta N \sigma/2, k = \alpha/k_0$ is the absorption coefficient.

The frequency dispersion of the imaginary part of the refractive index $k(\omega)$ is proportional to the absorption cross section and can be expressed as:

$$\sigma = \sigma_{max} \frac{\Delta v}{2\pi\left[(v_0 - v)^2 + (\Delta v/2)^2\right]} \frac{\pi \Delta v}{2} \tag{67}$$

It follows that

$$n(\omega) = 1.6 + \Delta n(\omega) = 1.6 + \frac{2}{\pi} P \int_{\omega_1}^{\omega_2} \frac{\omega'\left[k(\omega')\right]}{\omega'^2 - \omega^2} d\omega' \tag{68}$$

if $k(\omega)$ is odd function of ω and $\alpha(\omega) = \dfrac{2\omega k(\omega)}{c}$ is even function.

Assuming that $k(\omega)$ is different from zero only in a limited frequency band (ω_1, ω_2) (which is the case for the two emission/absorption Lorentzian bands), we can limit the integral to [66]:

$$\Delta n(\omega) = \frac{2}{\pi} P \int_{\omega_1}^{\omega_2} \frac{\omega'\left[k(\omega')\right]}{\omega'^2 - \omega^2} d\omega' \tag{69}$$

Also, this integral can be regularized in the following way

$$\Delta n(\omega) = \frac{2}{\pi} P \int_{\omega_1}^{\omega_2} \frac{\omega'\left[k(\omega') - k(\omega)\right]}{\omega'^2 - \omega^2} d\omega' + \frac{2}{\pi} P \int_{\omega_1}^{\omega_2} \frac{\omega' k(\omega)}{\omega'^2 - \omega^2} d\omega' \tag{70}$$

4.3.2 Model of silver

The permittivity of the metal can be expressed as Drude model:

$$\varepsilon_m = \varepsilon_\infty - \omega_p^2 / \left[\omega(\omega - j\gamma)\right] \tag{71}$$

where for silver $\varepsilon_\infty = 5$, plasma frequency $\omega_p = 1.37 \times 10^{16}$ rad/s and damping factor $\gamma = 27.3 \times 10^{12}\,\text{s}^{-1}$ [67].

The reflectivity (R) of silver as a mirror is also studied to estimate losses in the structures. Assuming a Febry-Perot cavity with all mirrors having the same reflectivity, we can compute the reflectivity based on the quality factor of the cavity.

$$R = \frac{2 + \left(\frac{2\pi n d}{\lambda Q}\right)^2 \pm \sqrt{\left[2 + \left(\frac{2\pi n d}{\lambda Q}\right)^2\right]^2 - 4}}{2} \tag{72}$$

Based on the relationship of $Q = \frac{2\pi n d}{\lambda} \frac{\sqrt{R}}{1 - R}$

Quality factor of the cavity Q can be expressed as:

$$Q = \frac{f_r}{2f_i} \tag{73}$$

Where f_r is the real part of the complex frequency and f_i is the imaginary part of the complex frequency.

4.4 Mode analysis

Using the transverse resonance method [68], the mode profile of the structures can be studied to retrieve the electric and magnetic field distribution. The proposed stucture in figure 20 can be studied as a five-layer structure as shown in Figure 22, with layers 1 and 5 assumed to extend to infinity in the z direction. Also, all the layers extend to infinity in the transverse directions.

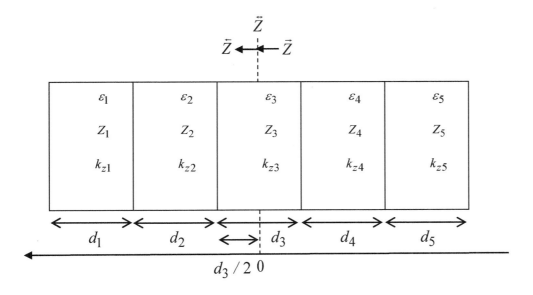

Figure 22. Structure under analysis.

For TE waves, the characteristic impedance of each layer can be expressed as:

$$Z_n = \frac{\omega\mu_n}{k_{zn}}$$

(74)

Where $k_{zn} = \sqrt{k_n^2 - k_t^2}$ and $k_n = \frac{\omega}{c}\sqrt{\varepsilon_n\mu_n}$, μ_n is the permeability of each layer and ε_n is the permittivity of each layer.

For TM waves the characteristic impedance of each layer can be expressed as:

$$Z_n = \frac{k_{zn}}{\omega \varepsilon_n}$$

(75)

The ABCD matrix analysis for cascade or transmission lines for each layer is introduced as follows for computing the electric field distribution in the structure shown in Figure 23.

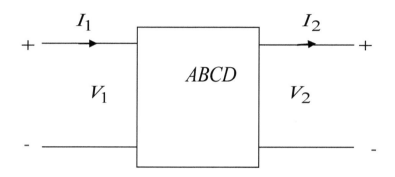

Figure 23. Configuration of ABCD matrix

The ABCD parameters are defined as:

$$\begin{pmatrix} V_1 \\ I_1 \end{pmatrix} = \begin{pmatrix} A & B \\ C & D \end{pmatrix} \begin{pmatrix} V_2 \\ I_2 \end{pmatrix}$$

(76)

$$T_n = \begin{pmatrix} A & B \\ C & D \end{pmatrix} = \begin{pmatrix} \cos(k_{zn}d_n) & jZ_n\sin(k_{zn}d_n) \\ j\frac{1}{Z_n}\sin(k_{zn}d_n) & \cos(k_{zn}d_n) \end{pmatrix}$$

(77)

where the input voltage of each layer can be expressed as V_1 and the input current can be expressed as I_1. The output voltage can be expressed as V_2 and the output current can be expressed as I_2. Z_n is the characteristic impedance of each layer and d_n is the thickness of each layer.

Using the ABCD matrix to analyze the structure in Fig. 22 to compute $\bar{Z}$ we get

66

$$\begin{pmatrix} V_3 \\ I_3 \end{pmatrix} = T \begin{pmatrix} V_1 \\ I_1 \end{pmatrix} = T \begin{pmatrix} Z_1 \\ 1 \end{pmatrix} I_1 \qquad (78)$$

$$T = T_3 T_2 = \begin{pmatrix} A_T & B_T \\ C_T & D_T \end{pmatrix} \qquad (79)$$

$$\bar{Z} = \frac{V_3}{I_3} = \frac{A_T Z_1 + B_T}{C_T Z_1 + D_T} \qquad (80)$$

Analogously for $\vec{Z}$

$$\begin{pmatrix} V_3 \\ I_3 \end{pmatrix} = T \begin{pmatrix} V_5 \\ I_5 \end{pmatrix} = T \begin{pmatrix} Z_5 \\ 1 \end{pmatrix} I_5 \qquad (81)$$

$$T = T_3 T_4 = \begin{pmatrix} A_T & B_T \\ C_T & D_T \end{pmatrix} \qquad (82)$$

$$\vec{Z} = \frac{V_3}{I_3} = \frac{A_T Z_5 + B_T}{C_T Z_5 + D_T} \qquad (83)$$

Then we define $\ddot{Z} = \vec{Z} + \bar{Z}$ and $\ddot{Y} = \bar{Y} + \vec{Y}$ and the even (with respect to the voltage) modes resonance condition is:

$\ddot{Y} = 0$ and the odd (with respect to the voltage) modes resonance condition is: $\ddot{Z} = 0$

Then, to find the modes, we fix ω and find k_{zn} by computing the zeroes of the previous equations as shown in the following paragraphs. Furthermore, knowing that

$k_{zn} = \sqrt{k_n^2 - k_t^2}$, $k_t^2 = k_x^2 + k_y^2$ we can find k_x and k_y.

Considering the geometrical symmetry in Fig. 22, it follows that $\ddot{Z} = \vec{Z} + \bar{Z} = 2\bar{Z}$ and

$\ddot{Y} = \bar{Y} + \vec{Y} = 2\bar{Y}$ and thus we only need to compute the zeroes of the numerator of $\ddot{Z}$ to

find odd modes, and the zeroes of the denominator of $\ddot{Z}$ to find even modes.

The condition of the even modes can be expressed as:

$$C_T Z_1 + D_T = 0 \tag{84}$$

The condition of the odd modes can be expressed as:

$$A_T Z_1 + B_T = 0 \tag{85}$$

$$T = T_3 T_2 = \begin{pmatrix} A_T & B_T \\ C_T & D_T \end{pmatrix} =$$

$$= \begin{pmatrix} \cos\left(k_{z3}\dfrac{d_3}{2}\right)\cos(k_{z2}d_2) - \dfrac{Z_3}{Z_2}\sin\left(k_{z3}\dfrac{d_3}{2}\right)\sin(k_{z2}d_2) & jZ_2\cos\left(k_{z3}\dfrac{d_3}{2}\right)\sin(k_{z2}d_2) + jZ_3\sin\left(k_{z3}\dfrac{d_3}{2}\right)\cos(k_{z2}d_2) \\ j\dfrac{1}{Z_2}\cos\left(k_{z3}\dfrac{d_3}{2}\right)\sin(k_{z2}d_2) + j\dfrac{1}{Z_3}\sin\left(k_{z3}\dfrac{d_3}{2}\right)\cos(k_{z2}d_2) & \cos\left(k_{z3}\dfrac{d_3}{2}\right)\cos(k_{z2}d_2) - \dfrac{Z_2}{Z_3}\sin\left(k_{z3}\dfrac{d_3}{2}\right)\sin(k_{z2}d_2) \end{pmatrix} \tag{86}$$

Thus, the condition of the even modes can be expressed as:

$$j\frac{Z_1}{Z_2}\cos\left(k_{z3}\frac{d_3}{2}\right)\sin(k_{z2}d_2) + j\frac{Z_1}{Z_3}\sin\left(k_{z3}\frac{d_3}{2}\right)\cos(k_{z2}d_2) + \cos\left(k_{z3}\frac{d_3}{2}\right)\cos(k_{z2}d_2) - \frac{Z_2}{Z_3}\sin\left(k_{z3}\frac{d_3}{2}\right)\sin(k_{z2}d_2) = 0 \tag{87}$$

In addition, the condition of the odd modes can be expressed as:

$$Z_1\cos\left(k_{z3}\frac{d_3}{2}\right)\cos(k_{z2}d_2) - Z_1\frac{Z_3}{Z_2}\sin\left(k_{z3}\frac{d_3}{2}\right)\sin(k_{z2}d_2) + jZ_2\cos\left(k_{z3}\frac{d_3}{2}\right)\sin(k_{z2}d_2) + jZ_3\sin\left(k_{z3}\frac{d_3}{2}\right)\cos(k_{z2}d_2) = 0 \tag{88}$$

The condition for TM even mode can be expressed as:

$$j\frac{\varepsilon_2 k_{z1}}{\varepsilon_1 k_{z2}}\cos\left(k_{z3}\frac{d_3}{2}\right)\sin(k_{z2}d_2) + j\frac{\varepsilon_3 k_{z1}}{\varepsilon_1 k_{z3}}\sin\left(k_{z3}\frac{d_3}{2}\right)\cos(k_{z2}d_2)$$
$$+\cos\left(k_{z3}\frac{d_3}{2}\right)\cos(k_{z2}d_2) - \frac{\varepsilon_3 k_{z2}}{\varepsilon_2 k_{z3}}\sin\left(k_{z3}\frac{d_3}{2}\right)\sin(k_{z2}d_2) = 0 \tag{89}$$

The condition for TM odd mode can be expressed as:

$$\frac{k_{z1}}{\omega\varepsilon_1}\cos\left(k_{z3}\frac{d_3}{2}\right)\cos(k_{z2}d_2) - \frac{k_{z1}}{\omega\varepsilon_1}\frac{\varepsilon_2 k_{z3}}{\varepsilon_3 k_{z2}}\sin\left(k_{z3}\frac{d_3}{2}\right)\sin(k_{z2}d_2)$$
$$+j\frac{k_{z2}}{\omega\varepsilon_2}\cos\left(k_{z3}\frac{d_3}{2}\right)\sin(k_{z2}d_2) + j\frac{k_{z3}}{\omega\varepsilon_3}\sin\left(k_{z3}\frac{d_3}{2}\right)\cos(k_{z2}d_2) = 0 \tag{90}$$

The condition for TE even mode can be expressed as:

$$j\frac{k_{z2}\mu_1}{k_{z1}\mu_2}\cos\left(k_{z3}\frac{d_3}{2}\right)\sin\left(k_{z2}d_2\right)+j\frac{k_{z3}\mu_1}{k_{z1}\mu_3}\sin\left(k_{z3}\frac{d_3}{2}\right)\cos\left(k_{z2}d_2\right)$$

$$+\cos\left(k_{z3}\frac{d_3}{2}\right)\cos\left(k_{z2}d_2\right)-\frac{k_{z3}\mu_2}{k_{z2}\mu_3}\sin\left(k_{z3}\frac{d_3}{2}\right)\sin\left(k_{z2}d_2\right)=0$$

(91)

The condition for TE odd mode can be expressed as:

$$\frac{\omega\mu_1}{k_{z1}}\cos\left(k_{z3}\frac{d_3}{2}\right)\cos\left(k_{z2}d_2\right)-\frac{\omega\mu_1}{k_{z1}}\frac{k_{z2}\mu_3}{k_{z3}\mu_2}\sin\left(k_{z3}\frac{d_3}{2}\right)\sin\left(k_{z2}d_2\right)$$

$$+j\frac{\omega\mu_2}{k_{z2}}\cos\left(k_{z3}\frac{d_3}{2}\right)\sin\left(k_{z2}d_2\right)+j\frac{\omega\mu_3}{k_{z3}}\sin\left(k_{z3}\frac{d_3}{2}\right)\cos\left(k_{z2}d_2\right)=0$$

(92)

Assume that $\mu_n=1$ for every layer.

Next we analyze the five-layer structure as shown in figure 22 with d_3 = 500 nm, $d_2=d_4=100$ nm and $d_1=d_5=\infty$ using the ABCD matrix method introduced before. There are two modes: M1 for guiding a mode at the emission frequency as a signal mode and M2 for exciting the erbium layer at the absorption frequency as a pump mode as shown in Figure 24.

Mode 1 is well guided inside the erbium at the emission frequency by imposing $k_t=0$ to solve for the complex frequency using ABCD matrix . Mode 2 is mainly guided in the erbium layer to solve for k_t. We can use it at the pumping frequency to pump energy to the erbium layer. We have both k_t and $-k_t$ solutions, but only the first one is reported in the dispersion diagrams.

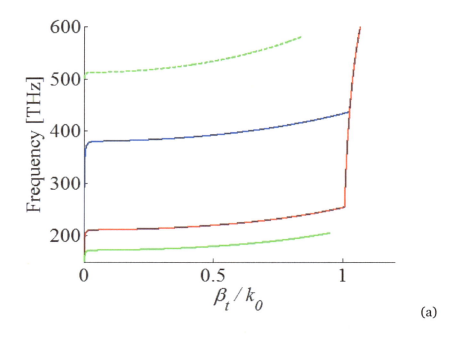

(a)

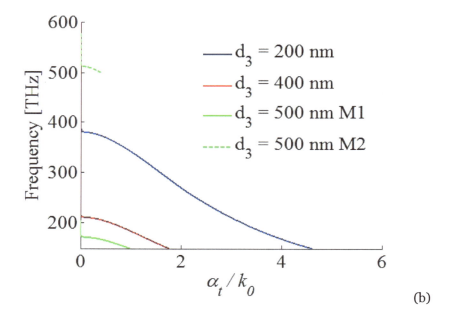

(b)

Figure 24. Dispersion diagram of different modes of the proposed structures.

(a)Propagation constants vs. frequencies.

(b) Attenuations vs. frequencies.

The electric field profile for Mode 1 at 1530 nm is shown in Figure 25:

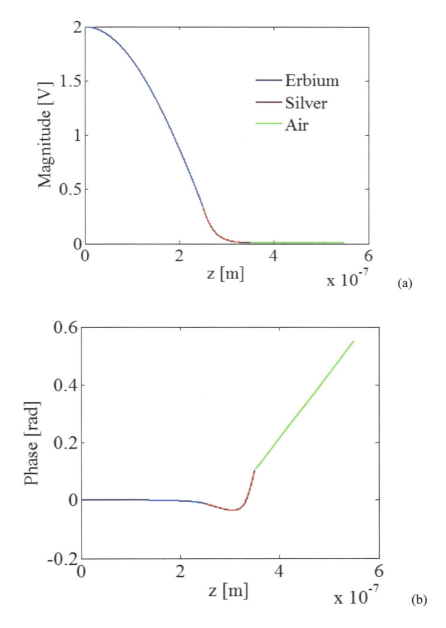

Figure 25. (a) Magnitude of electric field profile of mode 1 at 1530 nm .

(b) Phase of electric field profile of mode 1 at 1530 nm .

The electric field profile for Mode 2 at 521 nm is shown in Figure 26:

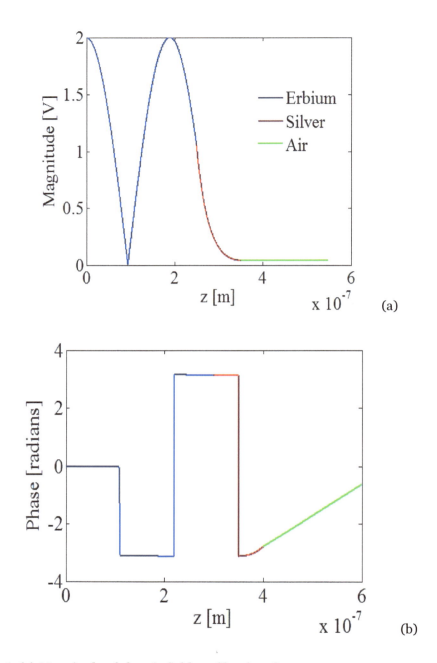

Figure 26. (a) Magnitude of electric field profile of mode 2 at 521 nm.

(b) Phase of electric field profile of mode 2 at 521 nm.

4.5 Simulation results

The net gain of the proposed device structure as shown in figure 20 can be computed by one round trip gain inside the cavity:

$$G = e^{2\Delta N \sigma_{em} d_g} R^4 \tag{93}$$

Where $\exp\left(2\Delta N \sigma_{em} d_g\right)$ represents the small signal power gain experienced in a round trip in the cavity ($\Delta N = N_2 - N_1$ is the population inversion), and R^4 represents the reflectivity or power loss due to the two silver mirrors. A net gain is achieved when $G \geq 1$.

Change of reflectivity with thickness d_m of the silver layer is shown in Figure 27. Reflectivity is 99.78%, 99.5% and 99.35% when $d_m = 40$ nm, 50 nm and 80 nm, respectively, and it remains almost constant at 99.34% for increasing thickness d_m. Here, in this study, $d_m = 100$ nm is selected since a minimum of $d_m = 80$ nm is needed to guide a mode in the erbium region.

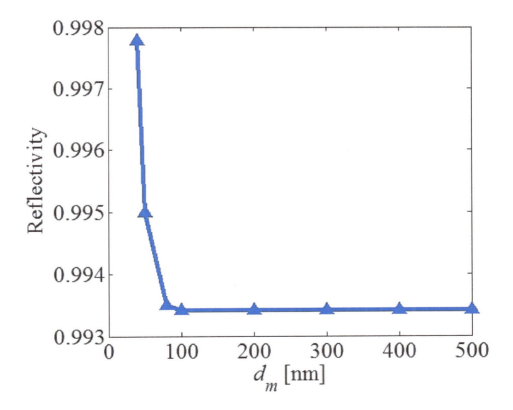

Figure 27. Silver reflectivity versus thickness d_m.

It can be observed from Fig. 28(a) that net gain ($G \approx 1.0055$) can be achieved in the cavity with thickness $d_g = 80\ \mu m$, and the population inversion versus z in this case is reported in Fig. 28(b); (only the portion from $z = 0$ to $z = 2\ \mu m$ is shown for illustration). Pump excitation is accounted for a single mode with magnitude of the electric field $|\mathbf{E}| \approx 0.65\ V/m$ at $z = 0$. Multiple pump-excited modes are supposed to create a more uniform population inversion profile.

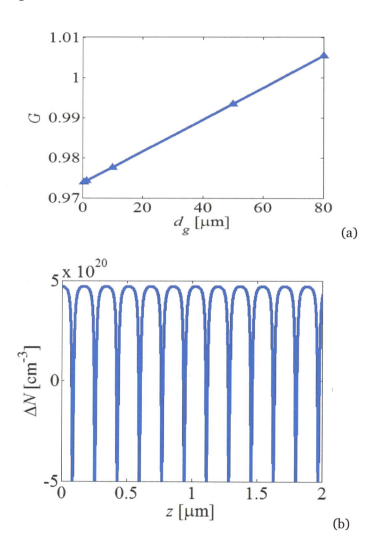

(a)

(b)

Figure 28. (a) G versus thickness d_g.

(b) ΔN (standing wave pattern) to achieve net gain for $d_g = 80$ μm (only portion from $z = 0$ to $z = 2$ μm).

4.6 Summary

We have shown the possibility of vertical emission through an erbium-based plasmonic-assisted structure. We proposed the design of an Er^{3+} doped Al_2O_3 layer sandwiched between two metallic layers and observed vertical emission at 1530 nm using side pumping. Metallic layers were used to guide the plasmonic pump mode (mainly confined in the active material layer) and acted as mirrors in the vertical direction to form a cavity resonating at 1530 nm. Er^{3+} doped Al_2O_3 was used as a gain medium and single mode excitation at both pump and signal were considered. With 80 μm Er^{3+} doped Al_2O_3 layer and 100nm sliver layers, a net gain in the vertical direction can be achieved. The proposed structure allows net gain without dealing with the high attenuations of electromagnetic waves in plasmonic structures. Other active materials with larger absorption cross sections may be used instead of erbium to reduce the thickness needed to achieve net gain.

Chapter 5

Characterization of micron-sized Er^{3+} doped particles

5.1. Introduction

Real-time optical imaging and tracking of submicron particles are attractive approaches for in-vitro biological sample imaging and for capturing transient properties of target objects in electro-mechanics. Different laser scanning microscopes, including fluorescence or scattering based mechanisms, have been proposed and illustrated for obtaining high-resolution optical images [69, 70] .Unfortunately, temporal resolutions of the above mentioned laser scanning microscopes are between microseconds and seconds due to the mechanical limitation of scanning methods and the data acquisition speed of detector arrays [71]. Recently, wavelength-division-multiplexing (WDM) based confocal microscopy has been demonstrated as a useful tool for optical imaging and detection using the space-wavelength mapping technique [72-74]. In addition, time-wavelength mapping can provide a unique solution for improving temporal resolution to realize real-time optical measurements [10, 75, 76] using a single-detector and single-shot measurement. The time domain profile of ultrafast RF (Radio Frequency) signals can be mapped to the wavelength domain; thus, the spectral shape can be retrieved directly into the time domain by using a real-time oscilloscope after a dispersive time stretching process [77]. The time-wavelength mapping technique also prevails over the slow-speed conventional spectrometers and allows real-time single-shot measurement of dynamic processes [78]. Recently, this technique has been implemented to detect highly reflective objects with sub-gigahertz resolution [79, 80]. In another field of interest, image correlation spectroscopy has proved to be a powerful tool of measuring dynamic processes and providing spatially resolved transient information in biological systems [81]. By using correlation functions, analysis of temporal and spatial correlations of image series can provide dynamic information such as diffusion coefficients and velocity vectors.

In this chapter, WDM based time–space-wavelength mapping is demonstrated to integrate space-wavelength mapping and time-wavelength mapping configurations into a single system to achieve real-time high-resolution optical measurements. Using this technique, we first present real-time optical imaging of a 5 μm polystyrene microsphere as calibration of the system. As a further proof of concept, fingerprint stains are imaged with up to 200 μm/line spatial resolution and a real-time acquisition rate of up to 1 line/50 ns. We also perform single-shot imaging, measurement of consecutive data points captured in a single measurement and real-time dynamics of micron-size Er^{3+} doped silica particles and their correlated movements by tracking them in a 20 μm imaging range. The image generated by the time–space-wavelength mapping system is compatible with algorithms developed for image correlation microscopy. Here, we illustrate detection and tracking of objects with 50 ns temporal accuracy by applying the algorithms of correlation spectroscopy.

This chapter is organized as follows: First, space-wavelength mapping and time-wavelength mapping techniques are introduced. Next, image correlation spectroscopy is introduced, and finally, real-time optical imaging and tracking of micron sized Er^{3+} doped silica particles by using space-timewavelength mapping are discussed in details.

5.2. Space-wavelength mapping

The space-wavelength mapping technique is proposed and implemented as the directing of different wavelengths to different lateral spatial positions. Recently, an axial WDM (chromatic) confocal imaging system has been investigated both theoretically and experimentally as shown in Figure 29. This system is implemented by using a low-cost sub-nanosecond super-continuum and space-wavelength mapping techniques.

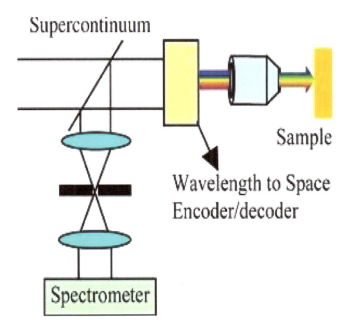

Figure 29. Schematic diagram of the wavelength division multiplexed confocal imaging system. (Figure courtesy: K. Shi [72])

Figure 29 illustrates the basic principle of a reflection-type WDM confocal microscope using the space-wavelength mapping techniques. Different wavelengths of the incoming supercontinuum are focused to different spatial locations by using a wavelength-to-space encoder/decoder and therefore interrogate multiple points on the sample in parallel. The reflected light is re-collimated by the same encoder/decoder. It is then spatially filtered by using a confocal pinhole to reject the out-of-focus background and scattered light. Since each wavelength carries information of a particular point, the images of an array of points on the sample can be obtained in parallel by detecting the spectrum of the reflected and spatially filtered light.

Unlike the wavefront or amplitude division multiplexed system (e.g., microlens array, Nipkon disk, or diffractive optical element based scanning system) the cross-talk noise between different points (i.e., different wavelength channels) is significantly suppressed, since different wavelengths are effectively separated and independently detected by the spectrometer. The cross-talk between different wavelength channels is related to the resolution of the spectrometer, which is determined by the pinhole size and the dispersive element (e.g., grating) used in the spectrometer.

WDM essentially reduces the three-dimensional scanning problem in conventional systems to a 2D problem. Specifically, X–Y–Z scanning can now be reduced to X–Y only (axial WDM or chromatic confocal system) scanning as shown in Figure 30(a) or X–Z only (lateral WDM confocal system) as shown in Figure 30(b) if the axial scanning (Z) or the lateral scanning (Y) is realized by wavelength division multiplexing.

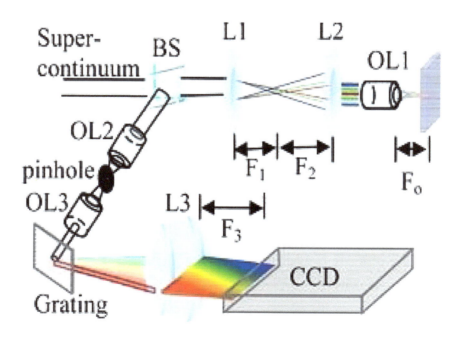

(a)

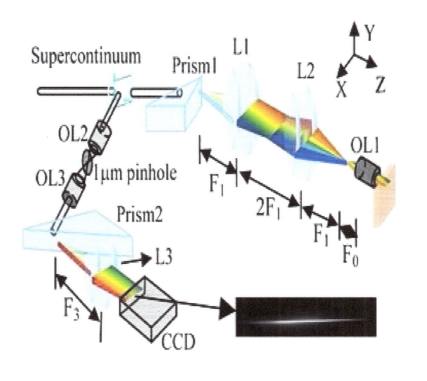

(b)

Figure 30(a). Schematic diagram of the axial WDM confocal microscope (Figure courtesy: K. Shi [72])

(b) Schematic diagram of the lateral WDM confocal imaging system (Figure courtesy: K. Shi [72])

5.3. Time-wavelength mapping

Due to the limited sampling rate of the electronic analog to digital converter (ADC), digitizing of ultrafast waveforms in real time is difficult to be realized and is a limitation for digital signal processing. Several promising techniques such as electro-optic methods and measuring of nonlinear interactions through optical cross correlation were proposed. However, interchannel mismatch errors are present in both techniques since they require a parallel array of detector/digitizer channels to capture the signal. Recently, approaches that permit digitization of ultrafast transients using a single channel are receiving interest because they avoid this limitation. One such approach, called time-stretch process, operates by stretching the time scale of an ultrafast transient, thus permitting its capture with a single digitizer channel.

The time-stretch process consists of time-wavelength mapping and wavelength-time mapping as shown in Figure 31. Time–wavelength (t–λ) mapping is performed by the combination of the chirped optical pulse and the electro-optic modulator. A gate signal is created by dispersing an ultrashort optical pulse into a dispersive medium like optical fibers. After the dispersion process, each temporal point across the pulse corresponds to a different frequency component. When the intensity of this chirped pulse is modulated by an electrical signal after the stretching, the time–wavelength transformation is achieved. Wavelength–time (λ–t) mapping is performed by a second dispersive medium followed by a photodetector. The modulated chirped pulse propagates through a second dispersive fiber. As a result, the temporal separation between individual frequency components increases, and the signal modulated onto the chirp pulse is stretched in the time. After the detection, a slowed-down representation of the high-frequency RF signal is obtained. A comprehensive and detailed treatment of the time-stretch theory can be found in [4].

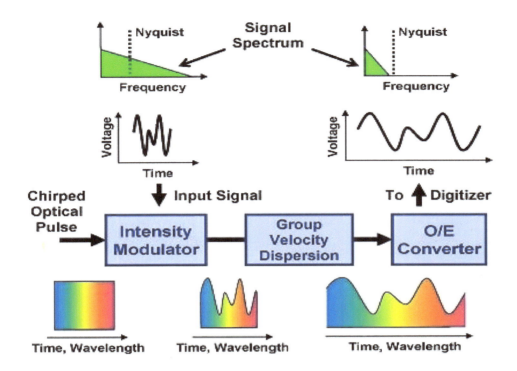

Figure 31. Conceptual diagram of the optical preprocessor. An ultrafast electrical signal is modulated onto the envelope of a chirped optical pulse which is further chirped and photodetected. As a result, the output electrical signal is time stretched, and therefore compressed in bandwidth, to within the Nyquist limit of a real-time oscilloscope. (Figure courtesy: A. Nuruzzaman [76])

5.4. Image correlation spectroscopy

Image correlation spectroscopy (ICS), developed by Petersen et al.[82] , is a mathematical image-processing technique that can be applied to any kind of image or stack of images. The basis of the ICS method is to calculate the spatial autocorrelation function of an image using two-dimensional fast-Fourier transform algorithms. The number and size of aggregates is extracted from the analysis of the spatial power spectrum. In a recent variation, space-time image correlation spectroscopy (STICS) [83], which is an extension of temporal ICS, allows temporal correlations between images collected in a time series as shown in Figure 32(a) and determines spatial correlations due to flow and other cellular processes in regions of living cells (2,6). This new approach allows the measurement of both diffusion coefficients and velocity vectors (magnitude and direction) for fluorescently labeled membrane proteins in living cells through monitoring of the time evolution of the full space-time correlation function. The STICS technique detects directed movements of macromolecules from the analysis of a time series of fluorescence images. The technique involves calculating the spatial-temporal correlation function as a function of the time lag between all possible sets of image pairs within an image time series as shown in Figure 32(b).

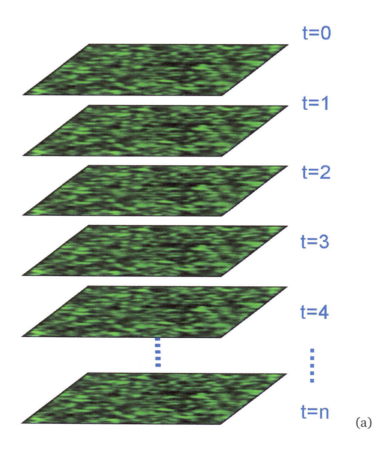

(a)

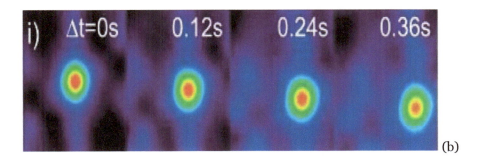
(b)

Figure 32 (a) Diffusion coefficient determined by temporal correlations using images collected in a time series. (Figure courtesy: P. W. Wiseman [83])

(b) Velocity vectors can be determined by spatial-temporal correlation using sets of images as a function of time. (Figure courtesy: P. W. Wiseman [83])

5.5. Space-time-wavelength mapping

Both space-wavelength mapping and time-wavelength mapping techniques can be utilized in the same system to achieve space-time-wavelength mapping. In time-wavelength mapping, each temporal point across the pulse corresponds to a different frequency component to realize real-time optical measurements using a single-detector and single-shot measurement. Space-wavelength mapping directs different frequency component to different lateral positions to reduce the dimension of scanning and cross-talk. By integrating these two techniques into one system, space-time-wavelength mapping is achieved to provide real-time optical imaging and tracking of micron sized Er^{3+} doped particles. Thus, in the system shown in Figure 33, WDM essentially reduces the two-dimensional scanning to one-dimensional sample scanning while information along the incident beam is provided by wavelength division mapping. As shown in Figure 33, a supercontinuum source is dispersed by the diffraction optics (gratings) to produce space-wavelength mapping in one spatial dimension. When the laterally dispersed incoming light encounters the target object, random amplitude modulation is created on the transmitted signal as in Figure 33. For two-dimensional micron-sized object optical imaging, the sample is scanned only in the dimension normal to the incident beam direction while the lateral information (x axis in Figure 33) is provided by the dispersed beam. By comparing the modulated signal with the stored background signal, we can extract the information regarding the position of the object and the density of the scatterers. Imaging and detection of the target object can be realized in real-time by retrieving the single-shot data from the time domain by a detection module of a single-detector and a real-time digital oscilloscope. For particle tracking, dynamic monitoring of micro-particles is achieved by first manipulating the particle moving within a 20 μm image frame along the incident beam direction controlled by a piezoelectric stage with the same setup as in the previously mentioned WDM based system. Transient displacements of the particle induce variations in the temporal waveforms due to the amplitude modulation in different wavelengths along the incident beam direction. The trajectory of the particle is recorded and processed using the correlation spectroscopy method.

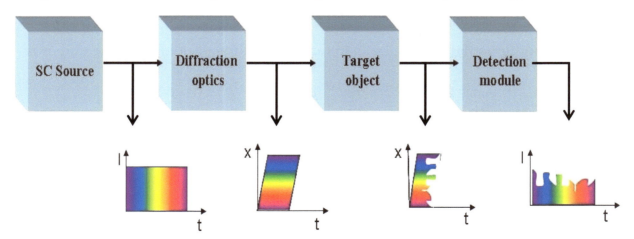

Figure 33. Conceptual diagram of real-time time–space-wavelength mapping system.

The experimental setup of the real-time high-resolution optical imaging and particle tracking system is shown in Figure 34. A 20 MHz fiber modelocked laser is used to generate a supercontinuum source with 50 nm bandwidth for imaging experiments. The generated light is then chirped by a grating based dispersion compensation module (1300 ps/nm) and hence time-wavelength mapping is produced. The temporally dispersed supercontinuum is subsequently dispersed in space by using a 600 lines/mm diffraction grating. At point "A" in Figure 34, an elliptical beam is shown, where each position along the x axis is mapped to a different color, arriving at different times. Then the beam is focused on the sample at point "B" by using microscope objectives OL1 and OL2 (numerical apertures of 0.65 and 0.85 for desired spatial resolution and high collection efficiency).

Polystyrene microspheres with 5 μm diameter are first used for the calibration of this setup. Then Er^{3+} doped glass particles are used as samples in this experiment. The samples are embedded in a thin polymer film and attached to a cover glass. Sample imaging is performed by monitoring the intensity of the transmitted light from the sample using an InGaAs detector. The presence of particles on the image plane induces amplitude modulation on different wavelengths, and these signals are captured in time domain by a high-speed real-time oscilloscope with 20 GS/s sampling rate. With only slight modification, this setup could for different-sized object imaging such as fingerprint stain imaging. The objectives lenses OL1 and OL2 in Figure 34 would be replaced with spherical lenses (f = 100 mm) for fingerprint object imaging.

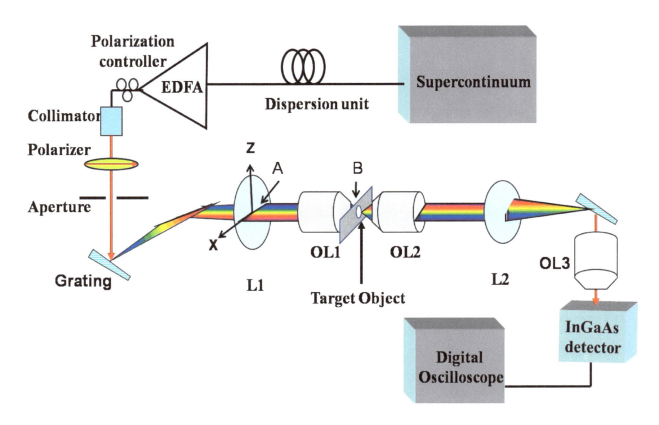

Figure 34. Experimental setup of real-time high-resolution optical imaging and particle tracking.

5.6. Real-time optical imaging of micron sized particles

Imaging and detection of the target object can be realized in real-time by retrieving the single-shot data from the time domain by a detection module of a single-detector and a real-time digital oscilloscope. A conceptual diagram of a real-time imaging system is explained in Figure 35.

For real-time two-dimensional micron-sized object optical imaging, the lateral spatial information (x axis at point "A" in Figure 34) is provided by a dispersed beam mapped to the time domain by space-time-wavelength mapping. Real-time optical imaging of objects is realized by scanning the sample only in the dimension normal to the incident beam direction (z axis at point "A" in Figure 34).   As shown in Figure 36, waveform "A" is the dispersed beam (waveform at point "A" in Figure 34) without encountering an object before the mechanical scanning. One dimensional mechanical scanning is achieved with 1 line/50ns capture rate. During the mechanical line scanning, different waveforms "B" and "C" which encounter different positions of the objects are retrieved by a detection module and a digital oscilloscope to generate a two dimensional image. When the modulated signals which vary with the encounter of different positions on the object during mechanical scanning (waveforms "B" and "C" in Figure 36) are compared with the stored background signal without encountering an object (waveform "A" in Figure 36) , we can extract the information regarding the shape of the object and the density of the scatterers. The row vectors of the 2D single-shot image as shown in Figure 36 correspond to different spatial locations (along the "x" axis in Figure 34), which are generated by a space–time-wavelength mapped single pulse. Column vectors represent the evolution of waveforms at different locations along the direction of one dimensional mechanical scanning, where each point is sampled at every T (50 ns), which is the pulse period. The whole image can be captured in a single-shot of N (N as a integer) pulses, which will generate N columns, and M rows, where M is the number of samples per period defined by the sampling rate.

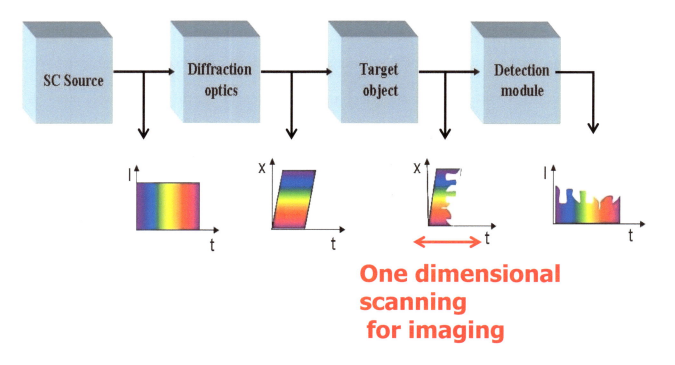

Figure 35. Conceptual Diagram of single shot single detector imaging system.

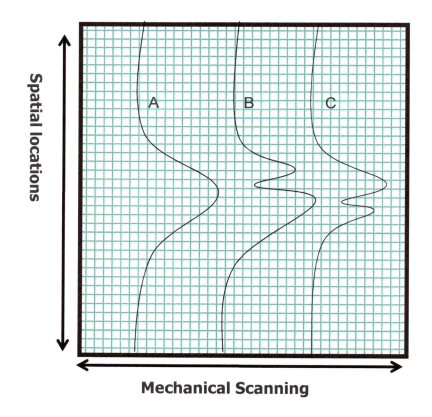

Figure 36. Illustration of real-time single shot single detector image generation.

Imaging capability of the system is evaluated by scanning different-sized objects in one-dimension. As a proof of concept, we first demonstrate 2D imaging of a 5 μm diameter polystyrene microsphere. This 2D image shows that a 5 μm microbead is resolved by the system as shown in Figure 37 (a). As a comparison, optical imaging of the microsphere captured by a Keyence digital microscopy is shown in Figure 37 (b). In this experiment, we show that microbeads of 5 μm diameter can be detected and imaged with 5 μm resolution. Here, the line capture rate is determined by the laser pulse rate, fixed at 1 line/50 ns.

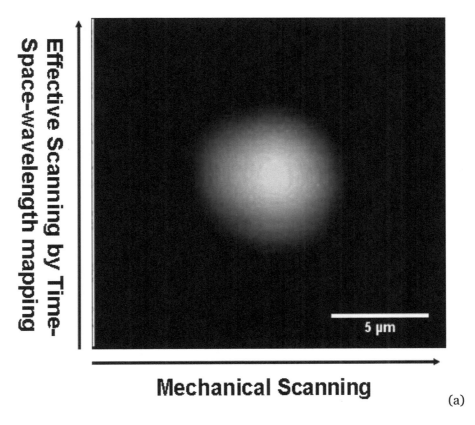

(a)

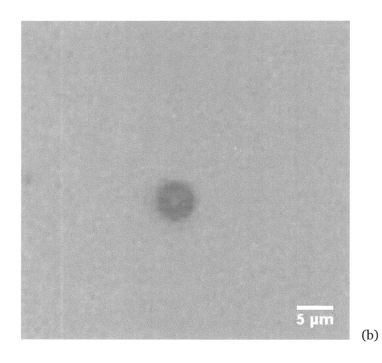

(b)

Figure 37. Imaging of a 5 µm polystyrene microsphere.

(a) Image generated by single-shot space–time-wavelength mapping technique.

(b) Image captured by high-resolution Keyence microscope.

The resolution of this system consists of the resolution imposed by the diffraction limit and the resolution imposed by the detection scheme in this system. The resolution imposed by the diffraction limit is shown in Eq. (1) below. NA$_{obj}$ is the numerical aperture of the objectives, and is calculated as 1.5 µm for k = 1.55 µm. In addition to diffraction limit, the detection system is limited in the spatial resolution due to RF filtering. The detection resolution of this scanning system is shown in Eq. (2) below. It is inversely proportional to the optical bandwidth ($\Delta\lambda$), the fiber dispersion (D) and the RF bandwidth (BW$_{RF}$) of the detector, and proportional to the beam width at object plane (d). The resolution of the system is the larger of:

$$\text{Diffraction limit} = 0.61 \frac{\lambda}{NA_{obj}} \qquad (94)$$

And

$$\text{Detection resolution} = \frac{d}{\Delta\lambda \times D \times BW_{RF}} \tag{95}$$

RF filtering can improve the detection resolution to d/44 by the optical bandwidth after fiber dispersion (22 ns) and the detection bandwidth (2 GHz) used in this system. Beam width at the object plane (d) can be controlled by the numerical aperture of the focusing objective lens. Hence, resolution of the system is mainly limited by the diffraction limit (1.5 µm) in this system. By using high numerical aperture lenses such as 80× objective lenses, resolution as small as 1 µm is achievable. The imaging system proposed clearly demonstrates that it can resolve sizes of objects with different order of magnitudes. As expected, increasing the scan area is feasible without losing the resolution by using larger bandwidth optical sources. Also, target objects of various profiles can be readily distinguished by this configuration. The application of this proposed scheme also includes detection of objects of arbitrary shapes. To further demonstrate the ability of this image system to detect arbitrary shapes, a single-shot image of a fingerprint stain of 2 mm × 1 cm area on a glass substrate is illustrated in Figure 38 using the same apparatus. Each 200 µm line can be clearly resolved in the image and one-dimensional information is acquired by mechanical scanning. In another application, random sized erbium doped glass particles (refractive index = 1.6) are also imaged using the above mentioned imaging system. A 2D image of micron-size erbium doped glass particle is constructed which has a size of approximately 15 um as shown in Figure 39.

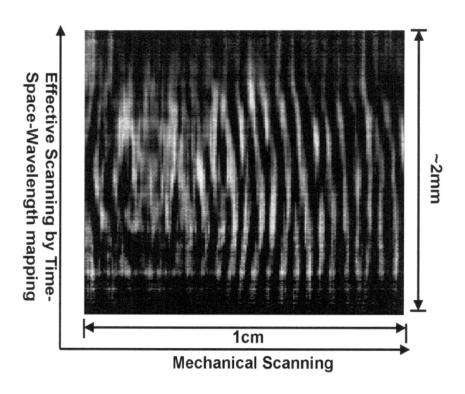

Figure 38. Single-shot 2D image of a fingerprint stain.

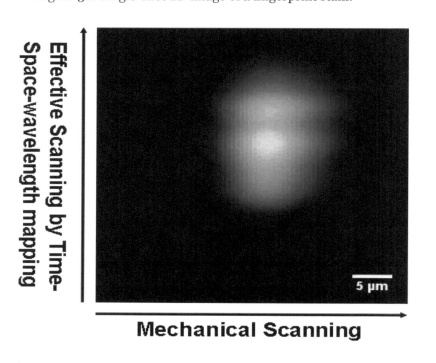

Figure 39. Image of ~15 μm random glass particles by single-shot space–time-wavelength mapping.

5.7. Real-time optical tracking of micron sized Er³⁺ doped silica particles

The conceptual diagram of a real-time particle tracking system is illustrated in Figure 40. In this system, an Er^{3+} doped silica particle is moving along the lateral direction (x axis at point "A" in Figure 34) and the lateral spatial information is provided by a dispersed beam, mapped to the time domain by space-time-wavelength mapping. As shown in Figure 41, waveform "A" is the dispersed beam (waveform at point "A" in Figure 34) without encountering a particle. During the particle movements, different waveforms "B" and "C" from which encounter the particle at different times are retrieved by a detection module and a digital oscilloscope. By comparing the modulated signals varying with time (waveforms "B" and "C" in Figure 42 (b)) with the stored background signal where no object was encountered (waveform "A" in Figure 42(a)), we can extract the information regarding the position of the object. Thus, real-time particle tracking is realized by comparing different waveforms changing over time. In order to improve the signal to noise ratio and to extract the dynamic information of the particle, a two-dimensional cross-correlation function is utilized by using background image and single shot data as shown in Figure 42.

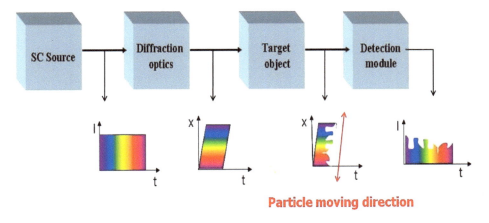

Figure 40. Conceptual Diagram of real-time particle tracking system.

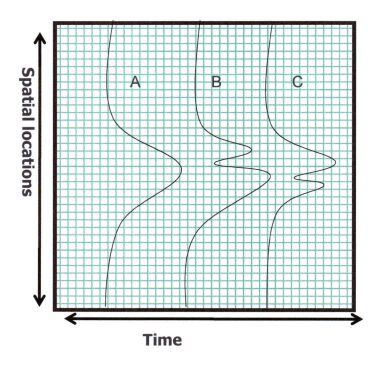

Figure 41. Illustration of real-time particle tracking image.

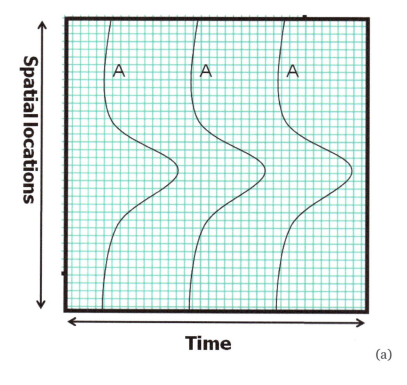

(a)

96

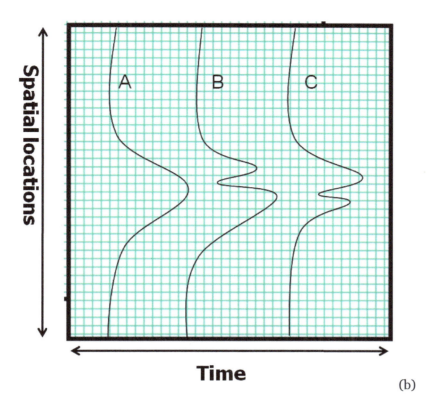

(b)

Figure 42 Cross-correlation of single-shot retrieved image of real-time tracking of a micron-sized glass particle.(a) Stored background signal without encountering an object

(b) modulated signals varying with time

Figure 43 shows a single-shot image of real-time tracking of a micron-sized Er^{3+} doped silica particle in a 20 ms time window with 50 ns temporal resolution and 5 µm spatial resolution. A sample of micro-size Er^{3+} doped silica (refractive index = 1.6) buried in a thin polymer film attached to a cover glass is mounted on a piezoelectric stage that is driven with a 1.5v peak to peak ramp function at 50 Hz. The sample movement is within 20 µm controlled by the stage. The row vectors of the 2D single-shot image correspond to different spatial locations, x, which are generated by a space–time-wavelength mapped single pulse. Column vectors represent the evolution of the particle at a specific location over time t, where each point is sampled at every T (50 ns), which is the pulse period. The whole image can be captured in a single-shot of N (N as an integer) pulses, which will

97

generate N columns, and M rows, where M is the number of samples per period defined by the sampling rate. The dynamic trace of the sample is clearly captured in the time domain and from spatial locations converted from variations in the spectral domain. Such data capture rate and tracking can be utilized in applications such as biophotonics and MEMS characterization where detection of correlated events along multiple points is useful.

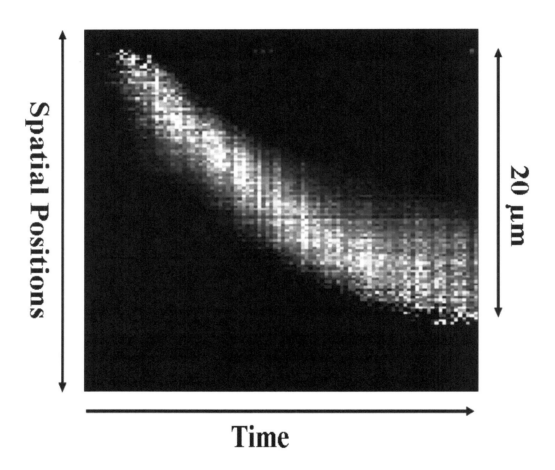

Figure 43. Single-shot retrieved image of real-time tracking of a micron-sized glass particle.

In order to improve the signal to noise ratio and to extract the dynamic information of the particle, a two-dimensional cross-correlation function is utilized in data post-processing. We can express each point in   single-shot captured image as shown in

Figure 44 (a) with particle movement, as $I_s(x, t)$ while x and t are spatial and time locations and the image has the dimension of $I_s(x_s, t_s)$. Similarly, each point in the single-shot background image as shown in Figure 44 (b) where there was no particle encounter can be defined as $I_r(x, t)$ and the reference background image has the dimension of $I_r(x_r, t_r)$. Let R(x, t) in Eq. (96) be the two-dimensional discrete cross-correlation function defined versus the spatial and time locations x and t respectively.

$$R(\xi, \tau) = \sum_{x=0}^{x_s-1} \sum_{t=0}^{t_s-1} I_s(x, t) \times I_r^*(x + \xi, t + \tau))$$

(96)

Where ξ is the spatial increment and τ is the time increment, and "I*" means the complex conjugate function. $0 \leq \xi \leq x_s + x_r - 1$, $0 \leq \eta \leq t_s + t_r - 1$.

In this system, the particle is moving uniformly and the trace of the shifted correlation peak can clearly represent the positional change of the particle ($\xi = v \times \Delta t, \tau = \Delta t$). By using correlation algorithms, the individual micro-particle is tracked as a single image, and its position, trajectory, magnitude of velocity and instantaneous displacement are determined from cross-correlation methods. A contour plot of the two-dimensional cross-correlation function of the particle movement is shown in Figure 45. The cross-correlation function retrieves the perfect line movement of the particle, which suppresses the noise, compared to Figure 43. These results show that the demonstrated imaging system is compatible with conventional spectroscopy techniques such as correlation spectroscopy [84, 85]. In image correlation spectroscopy, diffusion coefficients as well as spatially resolved dynamic information are provided by correlating between spatial points from a series of images. The space–time correlation function used in correlation spectroscopy can be expressed as in [86]:

$$r_{ab}(\xi,\eta,\tau) = \frac{\left\langle \delta i_a(x,y,t)\delta i_b(x+\xi,y+\eta,t+\tau)\right\rangle}{\left\langle i_a\right\rangle_t \left\langle i_b\right\rangle_{t+\tau}}$$

(97)

Where $\delta i_{a(b)}(x,y,t)$ is the intensity fluctuation in channel a(b) at space position (x,y) and time t. The same data can be captured by extracting the intensity variation from the image generated by space-time-wavelength mapping algorithm.

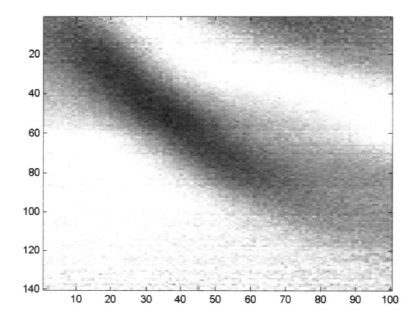

(a)

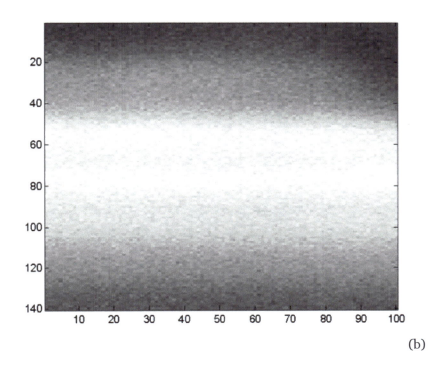

(b)

Figure 44 (a)Single-shot retrieved image of real-time tracking of a micron-sized glass particle.

(b) Background image without the presence of a a micron-sized glass particle.

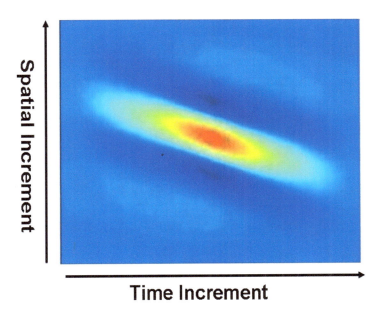

Figure 45 Contour plot of two−dimensional cross-correlation of the particle movement.

Here, we image dynamics of events occurring in a single line over a long time duration. Hence, the intensity at spatial location x expressed as I(t + nT) reveals the intensity variation at the spatial location x with a temporal accuracy of T, where T is the laser repetition rate of 50 ns and n is an integer. Similarly, we can capture information about multiple spatial locations (ie., multiple lines) in a single-shot image. Thus, by using conventional correlation algorithms such as cross-correlation algorithms, this system can identify correlated events along the image plane and detect instantaneous correlated events with temporal accuracy of T (50 ns).

5.8. Summary

We have characterized micron sized Er^{3+} particles by single-shot, single-detector high-resolution imaging and tracking. Imaging and tracking can be achieved by a time−space-wavelength mapping technique. We experimentally demonstrated single-shot imaging of a 5 μm Er^{3+} particle at a 1 line/50 ns capture rate. A correlation method was implemented to obtain the transient movement of the individual, 5um Er^{3+} particle. Although we have demonstrated feasibility for a single particle, the system can be easily optimized for real-time imaging and tracking of multiple micro-particles or arbitrary objects. We have also shown how existing spectroscopy algorithms can be utilized to obtain the dynamic flow information of particles. For simplicity and feasibility, this research focused on single-shot imaging of a single dimension. Future extensions of the proposed work may include single-shot 2D imaging by using a combination of multiple gratings and polarization multiplexing.

Conclusion

This dissertation describes the theoretical studies of planar structures with erbium doped regions which can be used for the fabrication of silicon compatible optical integrated circuits operating at 1.54 μm. This dissertation further includes a theoretical study of a vertical emitter structure consisting of Er^{3+} doped active material sandwiched between metal layers. Finally, this dissertation presents the characterizations of Er^{3+} doped particles with single-shot, single-detector high-resolution imaging and tracking.

Chapter 3 of this dissertation discusses the effects of design geometries and nonlinear losses on gain in silicon waveguides with erbium-doped Al_2O_3 regions. Performance of silicon waveguides with erbium-doped Al_2O_3 regions was limited by the upconversion and excited state absorption. We found that second-order upconversion is one of the main detrimental effects that prevent signal gain at high erbium concentrations. We compared the distribution of erbium ions over multitrench and single trenches, and found that the gain to nonlinear loss ratio was improved by the multitrench design. The multitrench configuration provides a 0.38 dB/cm higher signal amplification than the single-trench configuration. We also determined that the linear losses of the devices are mainly due to the fabrication processes. Future designs cannot ignore linear losses, so fabrication processes will need to be improved to provide ultimate high signal amplification.

Chapter 4 of this dissertation discusses an erbium-based plasmonic-assisted vertical emitter. The structure of an Er^{3+} doped Al_2O_3 layer sandwiched between two metallic layers is proposed and vertical emission at 1.53μm using side plasmonic pumping is observed. Metallic layers are used to guide the plasmonic pump mode which is mainly confined to the active material layer and acts as mirrors in the vertical direction to form a cavity resonating at 1.53μm. With 80μm Er^{3+} doped Al_2O_3 layer and 100nm sliver layers, we showed that net gain in the vertical direction can be achieved. In the proposed structure, pump and emission directions are orthogonal to each other, allowing net gain without encountering the high attenuation of the plasmonic mode for emission. In future studies, we believe that the size of the emitter may be reduced by using other gain materials with larger absorption cross sections to achieve a higher net gain.

Chapter 5 of this dissertation discusses the characterization of Er^{3+} particles by high-resolution imaging and tracking by single-shot and a single-detector. Real-time Imaging and tracking of Er^{3+} particles are achieved by a time–space-wavelength mapping technique. Single-shot imaging of a 5 μm Er^{3+} particle is demonstrated at a capture rate of 1 line/50 ns. Transient movement of a 5um Er^{3+} particle is obtained by a cross correlation method. For simplicity and feasibility, this research focused on single-shot imaging of a single dimension. By using multiple gratings and polarization multiplexing future studies should be able to extend this research to single shot, two dimension imaging and tracking.

References

[1]   G. Keiser, "Optical Fiber Communications," in *Wiley Encyclopedia of Telecommunications*, ed: John Wiley & Sons, Inc., 2003.

[2]   R. Soref, "The Past, Present, and Future of Silicon Photonics," *Selected Topics in Quantum Electronics, IEEE Journal of,* vol. 12, pp. 1678-1687, 2006.

[3]   H. A. Lopez and P. M. Fauchet, "Erbium emission from porous silicon one-dimensional photonic band gap structures," *Applied Physics Letters,* vol. 77, pp. 3704-3706, 2000.

[4]   K. Hattori, *et al.*, "Erbium-doped silica-based waveguide amplifier integrated with a 980/1530 nm WDM coupler," *Electronics Letters,* vol. 30, pp. 856-857, 1994.

[5]   B. Denis, "PERFORMANCES AND POTENTIAL APPLICATIONS OF ERBIUM DOPED PLANAR WAVEGUIDE AMPLIFIERS AND LASERS," 1997, p. FAW7.

[6]   M. J. Myers, *et al.*, "High gain short length phosphate glass erbium-doped fiber amplifier material," in *Optical Fiber Communication Conference and Exhibit, 2001. OFC 2001,* 2001, pp. WDD22-WDD22.

[7]   M. A. Noginov, *et al.*, "Compensation of loss in propagating surface plasmon polariton by gain in adjacent dielectric medium," *Opt. Express,* vol. 16, pp. 1385-1392, 2008.

[8]   M. Ambati, *et al.*, "Observation of Stimulated Emission of Surface Plasmon Polaritons," *Nano Letters,* vol. 8, pp. 3998-4001, 2008/11/12 2008.

[9]   J. S. Ploem, "Laser scanning fluorescence microscopy," *Appl. Opt.,* vol. 26, pp. 3226-3231, 1987.

[10]   J. Chou, *et al.*, "Time-wavelength spectroscopy for chemical sensing," *Photonics Technology Letters, IEEE,* vol. 16, pp. 1140-1142, 2004.

[11]   P. C. Becker, "Erbium-Doped Fiber Makes Promising Amplifiers," *Laser Focus World,* vol. 26, pp. 197-&, Oct 1990.

[12]   B. R. Judd, "Optical Absorption Intensities of Rare-Earth Ions," *Physical Review,* vol. 127, pp. 750-&, 1962.

[13]   G. S. Ofelt, "Intensities of Crystal Spectra of Rare-Earth Ions," *Journal of Chemical Physics,* vol. 37, pp. 511-&, 1962.

[14]   C. Strohhofer and A. Polman, "Absorption and emission spectroscopy in Er3+-Yb3+ doped aluminum oxide waveguides," *Optical Materials,* vol. 21, pp. 705-712, Feb 2003.

[15]   T. Kitagawa, *et al.*, "Guided-wave laser based on erbium-doped silica planar lightwave circuit," *Electronics Letters,* vol. 27, pp. 334-335, 1991.

[16]   P. Camy, *et al.*, "Ion-exchanged planar lossless splitter at 1.5 μm," *Electronics Letters,* vol. 32, pp. 321-323, 1996.

[17]   E. Snoeks, *et al.*, "Optical doping of soda‐lime‐silicate glass with erbium by ion implantation," *Journal of Applied Physics,* vol. 73, pp. 8179-8183, 1993.

[18]   G. van den Hoven, *et al.*, "- Net optical gain at 1.53 ?m in Er?doped Al2O3 waveguides on silicon," vol. - 68, 1996.

[19]   R. Brinkmann, *et al.*, "Erbium-doped single- and double-pass Ti:LiNbO₃ waveguide amplifiers," *Quantum Electronics, IEEE Journal of,* vol. 30, pp. 2356-2360, 1994.

[20]   W. J. Miniscalco and R. S. Quimby, "General procedure for the analysis of Er3+ cross sections," *Opt. Lett.,* vol. 16, pp. 258-260, 1991.

[21]   D. E. McCumber, "Theory of Phonon-Terminated Optical Masers," *Physical Review,* vol. 134, p. A299, 1964.

[22] F. Di Pasquale and M. Federighi, "Improved gain characteristics in high-concentration Er^{3+}/Yb^{3+} codoped glass waveguide amplifiers," *Quantum Electronics, IEEE Journal of,* vol. 30, pp. 2127-2131, 1994.

[23] L. R. Moorthy, *et al.*, "Judd-Ofelt parametrization and radiative transitions analysis of Tm3+ doped alkali chloroborophosphate glasses," *Optical Materials,* vol. 12, pp. 459-465, 1999.

[24] L. R. Moorthy, *et al.*, "Absorption and emission characteristics of Er3+ ions in alkali chloroborophosphate glasses," *Spectrochimica Acta Part A: Molecular and Biomolecular Spectroscopy,* vol. 56, pp. 1759-1771, 2000.

[25] G. N. v. d. Hoven, *et al., Upconversion in Er?implanted Al2O3 waveguides* vol. 79: AIP, 1996.

[26] P. G. Kik and A. Polman, *Cooperative upconversion as the gain-limiting factor in Er doped miniature Al2O3 optical waveguide amplifiers* vol. 93: AIP, 2003.

[27] N. Daldosso and L. Pavesi, "Nanosilicon photonics," *Laser & Photonics Reviews,* vol. 3, pp. 508-534, Nov 2009.

[28] L. Dal Negro, *et al.*, "Optical gain in silicon nanocrystals," *Optical Materials,* vol. 17, pp. 41-44, Jun-Jul 2001.

[29] H. S. Han, *et al.*, "Optical gain at 1.54 mu m in erbium-doped silicon nanocluster sensitized waveguide," *Applied Physics Letters,* vol. 79, pp. 4568-4570, Dec 31 2001.

[30] M. Lipson, "Guiding, modulating, and emitting light on silicon - Challenges and opportunities," *Journal of Lightwave Technology,* vol. 23, pp. 4222-4238, Dec 2005.

[31] X. C. Sun, *et al.*, "Toward a Germanium Laser for Integrated Silicon Photonics," *Ieee Journal of Selected Topics in Quantum Electronics,* vol. 16, pp. 124-131, Jan-Feb 2010.

[32] M. Dejneka and B. Samson, "Rare-earth-doped fibers for telecommunications applications," *Mrs Bulletin,* vol. 24, pp. 39-45, Sep 1999.

[33] C. E. Chryssou, *et al.*, "Improved gain characteristics in Er3+-doped alumina (Al2O3) channel optical waveguide amplifiers for WDM systems," *Fiber and Integrated Optics,* vol. 18, pp. 167-178, 1999.

[34] A. J. Kenyon, "Recent developments in rare-earth doped materials for optoelectronics," *Progress in Quantum Electronics,* vol. 26, pp. 225-284, 2002.

[35] K. Worhoff, *et al.*, "Reliable Low-Cost Fabrication of Low-Loss Al(2)O(3):Er(3+) Waveguides With 5.4-dB Optical Gain," *Ieee Journal of Quantum Electronics,* vol. 45, pp. 454-461, May-Jun 2009.

[36] J. D. B. Bradley, *et al.*, "Gain bandwidth of 80 nm and 2 dB/cm peak gain in Al(2)O(3):Er(3+) optical amplifiers on silicon," *Journal of the Optical Society of America B-Optical Physics,* vol. 27, pp. 187-196, Feb 2010.

[37] Y. C. Yan, *et al.*, "Erbium-doped phosphate glass waveguide on silicon with 4.1 dB/cm gain at 1.535 mu m," *Applied Physics Letters,* vol. 71, pp. 2922-2924, Nov 17 1997.

[38] Q. F. Xu, *et al.*, "Experimental demonstration of guiding and confining light in nanometer-size low-refractive-index material," *Optics Letters,* vol. 29, pp. 1626-1628, Jul 15 2004.

[39] V. R. Almeida, *et al.*, "Guiding and confining light in void nanostructure," *Optics Letters,* vol. 29, pp. 1209-1211, Jun 1 2004.

106

[40] R. Sun, *et al.*, "Horizontal single and multiple slot waveguides: optical transmission at lambda=1550 nm," *Optics Express,* vol. 15, pp. 17967-17972, Dec 24 2007.

[41] S. H. Yang, *et al.*, "Giant birefringence in multi-slotted silicon nanophotonic waveguides," *Optics Express,* vol. 16, pp. 8306-8316, May 26 2008.

[42] V. Donzella, *et al.*, "Effect of Si-nc to Er(3+) Coupling Ratio in EDWAs Longitudinally Pumped by Visible Broad-Area Lasers," *Journal of Lightwave Technology,* vol. 27, pp. 3342-3350, Aug 15 2009.

[43] V. Toccafondo, *et al.*, "Evanescent Multimode Longitudinal Pumping Scheme for Si-Nanocluster Sensitized Er(3+)-Doped Waveguide Amplifiers," *Journal of Lightwave Technology,* vol. 26, pp. 3584-3591, Nov-Dec 2008.

[44] C. Vassallo, "1993-1995 optical mode solvers," *Optical and Quantum Electronics,* vol. 29, pp. 95-114, Feb 1997.

[45] S. Kim and A. Gopinath, "Vector analysis of optical dielectric waveguide bends using finite-difference method," *Journal of Lightwave Technology,* vol. 14, pp. 2085-2092, Sep 1996.

[46] K. Saitoh and M. Koshiba, "Full-vectorial finite element beam propagation method with perfectly matched layers for anisotropic optical waveguides," *Journal of Lightwave Technology,* vol. 19, pp. 405-413, Mar 2001.

[47] W. Berglund and A. Gopinath, "WKB analysis of bend losses in optical waveguides," *Journal of Lightwave Technology,* vol. 18, pp. 1161-1166, Aug 2000.

[48] G. N. vandenHoven, *et al.*, "Upconversion in Er-implanted Al2O3 waveguides," *Journal of Applied Physics,* vol. 79, pp. 1258-1266, Feb 1 1996.

[49] P. G. Kik and A. Polman, "Cooperative upconversion as the gain-limiting factor in Er doped miniature Al2O3 optical waveguide amplifiers," *Journal of Applied Physics,* vol. 93, pp. 5008-5012, May 1 2003.

[50] S. F. Li, *et al.*, "A numerical analysis of gain characteristics of Er-doped Al2O3 waveguide amplifiers," *Optical and Quantum Electronics,* vol. 34, pp. 859-866, Sep 2002.

[51] B. Jalali, "Can silicon change photonics?," *physica status solidi (a),* vol. 205, pp. 213-224, 2008.

[52] T. K. Liang and H. K. Tsang, "Role of free carriers from two-photon absorption in Raman amplification in silicon-on-insulator waveguides," *Applied Physics Letters,* vol. 84, pp. 2745-2747, Apr 12 2004.

[53] E. K. Tien, *et al.*, "Influence of nonlinear loss competition on pulse compression and nonlinear optics in silicon," *Applied Physics Letters,* vol. 91, Nov 12 2007.

[54] A. Polman and F. C. J. M. van Veggel, "Broadband sensitizers for erbium-doped planar optical amplifiers: review," *Journal of the Optical Society of America B-Optical Physics,* vol. 21, pp. 871-892, May 2004.

[55] C. P. Michael, *et al.*, "Growth, processing, and optical properties of epitaxial Er(2)O(3) on silicon," *Optics Express,* vol. 16, pp. 19649-19666, Nov 24 2008.

[56] P. G. Kik and A. Polman, "Erbium doped optical-waveguide amplifiers on silicon," *Mrs Bulletin,* vol. 23, pp. 48-54, Apr 1998.

[57] P. Blixt, *et al.*, "Excited-State Absorption at 1.5 μm in Er3+-Doped Fiber Amplifiers," 1992, p. WE2.

[58] G. N. vandenHoven, *et al.*, "Net optical gain at 1.53 mu m in Er-doped Al2O3 waveguides on silicon," *Applied Physics Letters,* vol. 68, pp. 1886-1888, Apr 1 1996.

[59] F. Dipasquale and M. Federighi, "Modeling of Uniform and Pair-Induced up-Conversion Mechanisms in High-Concentration Erbium-Doped Silica Wave-Guides," *Journal of Lightwave Technology,* vol. 13, pp. 1858-1864, Sep 1995.

[60] M. C. Gather, *et al.,* "Net optical gain in a plasmonic waveguide embedded in a fluorescent polymer," *Nature Photonics,* vol. 4, pp. 457-461, Jul 2010.

[61] P. Berini and I. De Leon, "Amplification of long-range surface plasmons by a dipolar gain medium," *Nature Photonics,* vol. 4, pp. 382-387, Jun 2010.

[62] X. Zhang, *et al.,* "Observation of Stimulated Emission of Surface Plasmon Polaritons," *Nano Letters,* vol. 8, pp. 3998-4001, Nov 2008.

[63] M. P. Nezhad, *et al.,* "Room-temperature subwavelength metallo-dielectric lasers," *Nature Photonics,* vol. 4, pp. 395-399, Jun 2010.

[64] M. T. Hill, *et al.,* "Lasing in metal-insulator-metal sub-wavelength plasmonic waveguides," *Optics Express,* vol. 17, pp. 11107-11112, Jun 22 2009.

[65] A. E. Siegman, *Lasers.* Mill Valley, Calif.: University Science Books, 1986.

[66] J. R. Lincoln, *et al.,* "Spectroscopic Evaluation of the Vibrational Coupling of Er3+ Ions in Phospho-Aluminosilicate Fibers and an Explanation of Compositional Variations in Er-Yb 1.5-Mu-M Amplifier Performance," *Journal of Luminescence,* vol. 60-1, pp. 204-207, Apr 1994.

[67] F. Capolino, *et al.,* "Characterization of complex plasmonic modes in two-dimensional periodic arrays of metal nanospheres," *Journal of the Optical Society of America B-Optical Physics,* vol. 28, pp. 1446-1458, Jun 2011.

[68] L. Felsen and N. Marcuvitz, 1994.

[69] J. Enderlein, *et al.,* "Highly Efficient Optical Detection of Surface-Generated Fluorescence," *Appl. Opt.,* vol. 38, pp. 724-732, 1999.

[70] W. Denk, *et al.,* "Two-photon laser scanning fluorescence microscopy," *Science,* vol. 248, pp. 73-76, April 6, 1990 1990.

[71] M. A. Digman, *et al.,* "Measuring Fast Dynamics in Solutions and Cells with a Laser Scanning Microscope," *Biophysical journal,* vol. 89, pp. 1317-1327, 2005.

[72] K. Shi, *et al.,* "Wavelength division multiplexed confocal microscopy using supercontinuum," *Optics Communications,* vol. 263, pp. 156-162, 2006.

[73] D. Yelin, *et al.,* "Three-dimensional miniature endoscopy," *Nature,* vol. 443, pp. 765-765, 2006.

[74] D. Yelin, *et al.,* "Large area confocal microscopy," *Opt. Lett.,* vol. 32, pp. 1102-1104, 2007.

[75] J. Chou, *et al.,* *Femtosecond real-time single-shot digitizer* vol. 91: AIP, 2007.

[76] A. Nuruzzaman, *et al.,* "Time-stretched short-time Fourier transform," *Instrumentation and Measurement, IEEE Transactions on,* vol. 55, pp. 598-602, 2006.

[77] Y. Han, *et al.,* *Tera-sample per second real-time waveform digitizer* vol. 87: AIP, 2005.

[78] D. R. Solli, *et al.,* "Amplified wavelength-time transformation for real-time spectroscopy," *Nat Photon,* vol. 2, pp. 48-51, 2008.

[79] K. Goda, "Amplified dispersive Fourier-transform imaging for ultrafast displacement sensing and barcode reading," *Appl. Phys. Lett.,* vol. 93, p. 131109, 2008.

[80] K. Goda, *et al.,* "Serial time-encoded amplified imaging for real-time observation of fast dynamic phenomena," *Nature,* vol. 458, pp. 1145-1149, 2009.

[81] P. W. Wiseman, *et al.*, "Two-photon image correlation spectroscopy and image cross-correlation spectroscopy," *Journal of Microscopy*, vol. 200, pp. 14-25, 2000.

[82] N. O. Petersen, *et al.*, "Quantitation of membrane receptor distributions by image correlation spectroscopy: concept and application," *Biophysical journal*, vol. 65, pp. 1135-1146, 1993.

[83] P. W. Wiseman, *et al.*, "Spatiotemporal image correlation Spectroscopy (STICS) theory, verification, and application to protein velocity mapping in living CHO cells," *Biophysical journal*, vol. 88, pp. 3601-3614, May 2005.

[84] Q. Q. Ruan, *et al.*, "Spatial-temporal studies of membrane dynamics: Scanning fluorescence correlation spectroscopy (SFCS)," *Biophysical journal*, vol. 87, pp. 1260-1267, Aug 2004.

[85] E. Gratton, *et al.*, "Fluctuation correlation spectroscopy with a laser-scanning microscope: Exploiting the hidden time structure," *Biophysical journal*, vol. 88, pp. L33-L36, May 2005.

[86] B. Hebert, *et al.*, "Spatiotemporal Image Correlation Spectroscopy (STICS) Theory, Verification, and Application to Protein Velocity Mapping in Living CHO Cells," *Biophysical journal*, vol. 88, pp. 3601-3614, 2005.